SHERO'S JOURNEY

ALIZA BLOOM ROBINSON

Copyright © 2019 Aliza Bloom Robinson.

ALL RIGHTS RESERVED. This book contains material protected under International and Federal Copyright Laws and Treaties. Any unauthorized reprint or use of this material is prohibited. No part of this book may be reproduced or transmitted in any form or by any means, electronic or mechanical, including photocopying, recording, or by any information storage and retrieval system without express written permission from the author/publisher.

Paperback: 978-1-64184-227-3

ebook: 978-1-64184-228-0

Table of Contents

Introduction v

PART 1

Chapter 1 – The Dream. 3
Chapter 2 – A New Mission 15
Chapter 3 – For What Have I Come? 18
Chapter 4 – Randall. 22
Chapter 5 – Who am I? 27
Chapter 6 – Introducing the Invisible 32
Chapter 7 – Betrayal. 36

PART 2

Chapter 8 – The Lion .41
Chapter 9 – Remembering. 48
Chapter 10 – Shero's Role 52
Chapter 11 – Fraud 58
Chapter 12 – The Village. 65

Chapter 13 – Born Different 70
Chapter 14 – Inner Drive. 76

PART 3

Chapter 15 – Journeys 81
Chapter 16 – Love in the Face of… or RUN! 89
Chapter 17 – Finding Bliss 93
Chapter 18 – Frustrated 98
Chapter 19 – Separation. 104
Chapter 20 – Serve Creation 107
Chapter 21 – The First Awakening 118

PART 4

Chapter 22 – Role on Planet Earth 123
Chapter 23 – New Calling 130
Chapter 24 – Forgiveness. 134
Chapter 25 – Wise Man. 138
Chapter 26 – Leaving Alcivar 151
Chapter 27 – Humanity is Tough. 153
Chapter 28 – Shero Returns. 157
Chapter 29 – Meeting Again 160

Afterword. 163
About the Author. 165

Introduction

Welcome to Shero's Journey!

I'm so glad you have picked up this book. It is quite different than the other books I've written, in that it is a Spiritual Adventure. When attending a writing retreat in Hawaii, Shero appeared to me and showed me her story. She also indicated that her story is actually trilogy – this book being the first in the series.

Shero, is a hero – for planet earth. As a child she knows she is different and can't quite figure out how or why. As it turns out, at the beginning of this book, which is really towards the end, she is different. She's been born from a different dimension – the Star Seed planet, for the purpose of healing our planet. In this first book, she is faced with a (s)hero's journey with dragons, and lions and other challenges showing up in the forms of human emotions; fear, rage, shame, betrayal. It is in the overcoming of these challenges and the embracing her humanity that Shero is prepared for her soul's purpose.

As you will quickly notice, there are two threads in this story. One is in regular font and is present and real time. The second is the italics portions of the story, which are the journeys that Shero has. Her journeys are sort of like dreams, but more like shamanic journeys, where she travels through different dimensions of time, space and consciousness.

Settle back, open your mind and enjoy the adventure through Shero's Journey!

With much love,
Aliza

PART 1

••• 1 •••

The Dream

SHERO MARVELED AT the call. For more than a decade she and her friend had been estranged and now, in a single and simple phone call, it was changing. They made plans to meet later that very day. Shero was now sitting on a bench, watching the steady waves roll gently onto the beach. They reminded her of the continuity of life and the ever-invisible power behind all things. The sky was a light powder-blue; the water a deep turquoise. The day was magnificent; her heart was full and her mind a bit blown away. There was so much to process as old memories and feelings arose. She could feel an inner journey about to begin; one that was calling her so deeply. Shero left the beach and returned to her room. Her inner journeys would cause her to fall fast asleep, like being taken out of consciousness and into a deeper-than-dreaming state. She would often lose all sense of time, almost as if being in a different dimension. Her experiences in the journey state were as real as any life experience. She set the alarm as she laid down on her bed so she would be sure to be awake in time to meet her long-lost friend. Sometimes her journeys were only a few minutes of real time yet could be hours or days in the experience.

She closed her eyes and began to be pulled into a journey; a type of dreaming but a dream that was more real than reality.

In the dream she was falling from an unknown place to another unknown place. It was a slow-motion free-fall with no speed and no fear. It was a bit like floating but with a sense of movement down, down, down.

"Where am I? What is happening?" Shero wondered.

The falling slowed even further; it was as if she were going through layers or dimensions of consciousness. She felt definite differences in the tiers.

She noticed the layers getting denser and then lighter; there appeared to be no pattern, just gradual distinctions.

Then she landed on a beach on a planet she did not yet recognize. It appeared like an Earth beach, but it felt different. The density was different. The sand glistened, the water shone, the air fairly sizzled with particles of oxygen and more.

Shero wondered where she was and what was happening. She felt open and receptive – and surrendered. She became curious and knew something big was about to happen.

As Shero walked along the pink sands of this beach she came to a sitting place. It was like a park bench but very other worldly; something out of the Jetson's television program from when she was a child. She sat on it and the bench conformed to her body.

It appeared to have a control panel, but she didn't know what it was for. She sat relaxed, alert, and aware of herself and her surroundings.

In the distance a figure approached. It was tall and appeared friendly. As it approached Shero's curiosity increased; she felt drawn to this figure, drawn to this man. Was it a man? Was she on Earth? No, it didn't seem like it. But his image appeared as a man. A wise man, a guide, or a sage, perhaps? She welcomed his presence and he welcomed hers.

"I'm so glad you came; we've been waiting for you."

"Really?" she said. "Okay, good," she thought; out loud she asked, "Where am I?"

"You are in the multi-dimensions — the space between the worlds. We call it Star Seed."

"What am I doing here?"

"You have come for your next assignment. Your next awakening. You are being welcomed to the tribe of Star Seeds. You have done your work alone to our satisfaction; now it is time to meet the others. Come along with me."

She stood, and together they walked along the beach to a pathway that led inland. It was well groomed, beautiful, lush; not a forest, not exactly tropical. It was unfamiliar yet almost recognizable. She couldn't identify any plant but recognized a scent. It was a bit ozone-ish with a slight scent of rose. It was familiar.

"I know this smell," she said.

"Yes," her guide replied. "You smell this when we are present; we let you get a whiff of it whenever you need support or are feeling a bit overwhelmed. It is our reminder to you that you are not alone; that we are present and are with you always."

"But who is 'we?' Who are you?"

"We are the council of spirit. You named us yourself. Remember when you did?"

Suddenly, she did remember. It had been years prior when she was doing what she came to call her spiritual initiation work in Joshua Tree, California. She recalled she was clearly supported by a council of spirits – invisible to the physical eye; yet so very present. Shero hadn't consciously called on them for years, figuring that was a stage and now she had surpassed them.

The guide laughed even before she spoke. "Yes, we are they. Yes, you are connected to us for all time and there was a time you were more consciously aware of us."

They continued their walk. The path felt vaguely familiar but not completely. Shero didn't recognize the place, yet it seemed like she should have.

They came to a clearing where there was a gathering in place.

It appeared to be a welcoming party; they began to cheer and clap and welcome Shero into their presence. She was humbled, honored, and a bit embarrassed by the attention. She stood in awe and wonder. They appeared to know her; they were acting as if she'd been away for a long journey and was returning. It was a homecoming.

Shero simply noticed what she noticed as she was greeted by man, woman, child and all. They knew her; why didn't she know who they were? Why did she feel left in the dark? They were celebrating and thrilled at her arrival and they obviously knew she was on her way.

"Fascinating," Shero thought. She'd been on enough of these journeys to know that something would be revealed; that it would all fall into place.

An older woman who appeared to be in her '80s appeared and order came over the crowd. Everyone sat as she approached the center of the circle. "We welcome back to us our beloved Shero. We witness your journey; we honor your presence and we are thrilled at your arrival."

Shero stood still stunned, not understanding the underlying theme of this homecoming. She thought, "I don't recognize these people; I don't recognize the energy field or the wise woman. How can I be returning when I didn't know I was ever here?"

There was more talk, cheering, and celebration. The people broke into cheers that became song. The song led to dancing. Shero was caught up in the singing and dancing; caught up in the presence and the power of an energy field that was pure love, adoration, and respect.

The party continued; the people were singing, dancing, and celebrating for hours, until in one moment the old wise woman spoke again. With authority, but not loudly, she said, "Thank you everyone for being here; it is time for Shero and I to talk." Immediately the crowd quieted and scattered into the foliage; leaving only the guide, the wise woman, and Shero. There appeared a circle of three chairs. Wise one motioned Shero to sit; the guide followed.

"You may have questions," the woman began.

"Yes, I do."

"But first I want to personally welcome you home. I want to personally welcome you to the fold."

"Home? But where am I, what am I doing here? Who are you?" Shero demanded.

"We have been with you since the beginning of your journey. We sent you into the world as a seed, as a thought possibility.

You thought you were human, but truly you are one of us. We are Star Seed beings. I am Ulima, keeper of the Star Seed People."

Shero studied Ulima; she was translucent in her being with beautiful snow-white hair pulled into a top bun; she was not tall, but not small either; she appeared to be as fit and energetic as a young woman and carried herself with the regal elegance of one who knows her place in the world as a leader.

"You are our experiment and our gift to humanity. You were consciously part of the plan and choose the role yourself. Soon you will begin to remember. We had to eliminate your memory so you could fully experience being human. For it was in living as human that you would and could impact the planet.

"We are the guardians of planet Earth. We are the Melchizedek clan of Star Seed and you are one of us. It was your mission to live among humans; to understand and to bring a new understanding of possibilities and potential to humanity.

"We have been with you always. You were assigned Michale as your Guide, to watch over you, to be with you, to be accessible and to report back to us. We were keeping you safe even as you walked as a human through humanity on planet earth. . . .

"Part of the agreement was a complete wipe-out of your memory, even of Michale.

"I'm pleased to make the official introduction. Michale, please meet Shero. Shero, please meet Michale."

Shero gazed into the Guide's eyes and he became familiar. "I remember you. I remember when I was a child, so lost and alone, knowing in my bones that I did not belong on that planet; that although I had a loving family, they did not understand me. That I did not fit there.

"You would come to me in the night and hold me. Remind me I was okay, that all was well and that I had a mission to do. I forgot about you; but now I'm remembering. I'm recognizing you.

"And that scent – the almost just-beyond-my-awareness rose smell. No one else could smell it, but I did. As a child I would ask others. They always denied it and told me I had an overactive imagination. I used to dream of this place, then one day those dreams stopped."

Michale came to her with a huge smile of recognition and hugged her. "Welcome back, my Shero."

Shero continued looking at him as memories flooded her awareness; memories of being connected, safe, and seen. She tore her eyes away from Michale as Ulima continued speaking in a melodic rhythm that calmed her soul.

"We wanted you to know you were safe; that you were not alone, but you were so connected to the dreams that you were not becoming fully human; you were not of the Earth and you were starting to live not of the Earth as well," Ulima said.

"We had gotten you through your young years as a child and it was time for you to be on your own. For the plan could not work if you thought you weren't human or if others realized you were not.

"So, you became human. We sent you as a seed; we choose your parents and family as best we could, and you were conceived as a divine idea in their minds. You were birthed as a human with Star Seed potential.

"Here on the Star Seed planet all we have is love, compassion, kindness. We do not have the polarity found on Earth. The polarity is the way of experience. In order to come to experience *love you must first experience the opposite, or absence of that same love. To experience forgiveness, you must have been betrayed. To experience anything, you must have the polar opposite. In order to make the greatest impact on Earth you had to be human and experience all that humanity experiences. In that, we had to let you experience separation.*

"Now, no longer. Now the mission is changing; the calling is different."

Ulima continued in a soothing, almost sing-song voice, "On Earth you were loved, although never understood. While we made you as human as possible you carried with you the Star Seed. The potential for remarkable things. It has been with you always.

"Now, however, you are ready to come home; to be reunited with your true family so that you can continue your work with humanity at a new level.

"This is why we welcome you home. Your presence, your brilliance, your light, is making a difference. You are processing through the emotions and experiences of humanity with great grace.

"Welcome home, Shero.

"You must have so many questions, but let's leave them for tomorrow. For today, be among the environment here, be with the people here and bask; simply open to receive their love and recognition. Open to receive, then sleep well.

"Tomorrow is another day and we will be here to answer all of your questions then. Until then, remember; job well done. Rest easy, my dear."

Shero left the circle. She wondered about this place, the Star Seed planet, as she wandered around exploring. She admired the foliage, the scents, the air that was different from that of home. She didn't know what home was – here, or planet Earth. Earth still felt like home.

She felt the energy, the light, the presence of those around her. Shero leaned into the honor they had for her; the thrill they all had in meeting her and being in her presence.

No one asked specific questions, nor did she; they communed at a heart level. There were no words; there was only love. Love that with each passing moment washed over her being. If love on earth was pink the love here was a brilliant magenta, glimmering, shimmery particles of pure essence. It was similar and totally different. It was beautiful and humbling.

Shero's heart was bursting open yet again into the magenta glistening presence of acceptance. That was part of what was different; it was acceptance in a way that she'd never felt in her life as a human. It was more than acceptance with love; it was respect; it was deep and pervasive.

Love wasn't a good enough word, but there was no other.

She walked, and talked, she connected. She opened herself fully and was recognized. She felt entirely at home. "I am home!" she realized. "Oh, my heart and soul are at peace. I'm home. I'm home. I'm home."

As if she'd never been on Earth. As if she'd never been before in her skin. She wondered why her skin here was so luminous. She wondered why her body here was different. Relaxed, at peace, at ease. "Oh," she realized, "this is the way of the Star Seed people."

It was time to rest; another one took her to her resting place. It was simple yet elegant; it was peaceful and as she lay down on the bed it conformed to her body like a blanket of foam. Like a bubble of love; as Shero lay down her head, she fell into a deep, restful sleep. She slept without moving, without dreaming, until the first morning light.

Shero awoke feeling rested and peaceful. She stretched and the bed released her; lifted her to standing. She stretched again noticing her body; she felt taller, stronger, more flexible than ever in her life. She was losing the density of human form and becoming lighter. She could feel it in herself; she could sense it as the energies of density lifted.

Shero walked outside and headed to the beach for her morning meditation. The birds were singing; it felt like a song just for her. The air was fresh; although low in the sky, the sun was bright and luminous. She was happy in the very cells of her being. She belonged here. She was home; the sense of relief, the sense of surrender was palpable, there was no effort in it. She was home. She was at peace.

The beach was empty. Shero sat and entered her meditation. Instead of "doing" meditation that morning, she became it. She became each breath she took. She became the various parts of her body as she scanned them. She became the sand on the beach and the water in the ocean. She became the breath she breathed. She became the particles of each thing she became aware of.

Then she became the wave from which the particle arose. She was one with all that was; an infinite possibility. She experienced the very source of creation as herself. She was infinite. Her body fell away; the edges of everything she knew herself to be dissipated, dissolved and she was one. She was the Earth and the sun, this planet and all things.

Shero journeyed from the beginning of time to the infinite; from the beginning of creation to the very ends of the earth; the *very edges of the cosmos. She expanded and was illuminated as One. She floated, and soared, she flew and continued expanding. She was not only "at" home, she "became" home.*

In the place of the wave Shero was infinite possibilities and each one had its path. She saw the infinite possibilities of humanity awakening. She saw the possibilities of a new Earth, either on that planet or another. She saw the other planets, infinite numbers of them, flying through the cosmos. She saw universes and stars and black holes. She reached to the very edge of consciousness and even there sensed the potential future that not had yet been dreamed into existence. She saw, felt, and became Creation itself as a miracle, as magic, as mystery all rolled into one. In the journey that continued on and on, Shero saw so many choices. So many possibilities, so many potentials. Each with its story line; each with its own opportunities for what was an adventure without the challenges.

Each story line had the similar theme of forgetting and remembering. It was expanding, contracting, and expanding again. It was ever expansive except for the choices that locked in contraction.

Shero was unaware of how long she journeyed within her journey, but then she was back, sitting on the Star Seed beach. One with the sky, the water, the sand, the earth. One with all that is. She felt herself shift from the wave of pure potentiality back into the particle called her being. Not her body so much as her being. She was renewed and refreshed. She was reignited and rejuvenated. She sat there looking at the beauty of the surroundings for quite some time. She enjoyed every moment, every movement, every sound and breath of breeze. Shero stood and walked into the shimmering, glimmering waters of the ocean.

It was warm and refreshing, just a degree or so below her body temperature. It was buoyant; she walked into the water but could just as easily been walking on the water. She dove down deep and noticed she could breathe under this water. Shero floated and played; a dolphin appeared to play with her. She swam with the dolphin, copying its movements and dance. It played with her; it invited her to swim alongside until she was fatigued and then was invited to hold onto its fin as it took her for a ride. Shero became the dolphin. She merged with it and was it as they danced and played and frolicked around. It jumped into the air, spinning as it entered the water; it enjoyed itself as much as Shero enjoyed it. It was another communion of oneness in which there was no separation.

They played and danced and jumped for what seemed like hours and then it was complete. With utmost gratitude and appreciation for their time together, they bid farewell as the dolphin dropped Shero at the beach once more.

As Shero rose and walked out of the water her guide, Michale was there waiting and watching her. He observed, "You met Randall – did you enjoy Oneness with all that is?"

••• 2 •••
A New Mission

"ULIMA WISE ONE woman is awaiting you. A feast is being served and she will have you in her private garden. Please stop by the food and choose the items of your desire," Michale said as he escorted Shero back up the path to the gathering area.

Shero walked to a food area; it was an ultimate buffet of fresh fruits most of which she had never seen before. It was beautiful in color and display, the scents heavenly.

The wise woman was waiting for her in a beautiful garden setting. It was different from yesterday, and equally beautiful. She rose and greeted Shero with an embrace. It was a hug, but so much more — it was a full-body and full-energy field hug. It welcomed all of Shero into her space, into her environment and into her consciousness. Shero felt greeted like royalty; it was an honoring she didn't yet feel deserving of or understand.

They sat and ate in companionable silence. The tea was poured; the plates removed. Ulima invited Shero into silence. It was easy, it was complete, it was surreal. The silence was full of nothingness; it was purity of spirit, purity of energy.

They merged into the silence and into oneness, a Oneness of which she'd only begun to experience in her morning on the beach; a Oneness of which Shero had not even glimpsed in her time on planet Earth, as she was beginning to call it.

A few hours ago, it was home; now it became planet Earth.

Then Ulima spoke. She said, with all the love in the universe, "Thank you for doing what you are doing. You are making a great and grand impact on the world as we know it. For everything that happens on planet Earth is impacting the universe as it is.

"We bring you here today because you are coming to a crossroads. The work we sent you to do is changing as the world is changing, and you have a choice again. We have been with you; the silent impulses you follow are subtle signals from us.

"The life you have lived has been full and rich with experiences. The lessons you have learned about surrender, love, acceptance, and non-resistance, will serve you and humanity well. The lessons you have taught the humans you have been in contact with have served you well also.

"You model, you teach, and your impact is far greater than you can imagine.

"Now, however, you also are at a junction of choice.

"First, let us take some time to answer any questions you might have. Ask me anything at all and I'll be with you."

At first, Shero had no questions. She just was basking in the moment, basking in the energy. She was full and complete.

Nothing missing, nothing in her mind or on her heart. They sat together for a time in the silence.

Then her questions began: "Why and what and how come? What is the suffering all about? Why me? What really is my role? How could you leave me there all alone? Why didn't you come sooner?" The humanity that Shero was came flying through with a barrage of questions about who, what, when, where and why . . . especially, so much why.

•••3•••
For What Have I Come?

ULIMA LET SHERO *ramble on for a time with a gentle smile. As Shero threw questions at her so fast and furiously, there was no time for answers. Then Shero paused. The Wise Woman smiled and asked, "So what is your real question?"*

"For what have I come?" Shero responded. It seemed the over-compassing question. "You celebrate my work and yet I do not feel successful. I have been only a slight pebble thrown into the sea of existence. How can what I've done been of any impact at all?"

Ulima took Shero's hands in hers and looked deeply into her eyes. "This is the work my dear. It only takes one to change the projection of humanity. And you are one of us, the Star Seed people; sent to the earth to be a seed. A seed of possibility in a world of potential.

"The work of humanity lies in undoing the illusion of separation. So many things you've walked through you are doing not only for your own consciousness, your own awareness, but for all of humanity. As you face the fears of humanity you are clearing a cosmic pattern that has been put in place over millennia; you are interrupting an energetic cycle that has kept humanity in bondage.

"They do not even know what bondage is, they are so immersed. Remember Earth's story of Moses who was called to free the people of Egypt? God, Yahweh, called him. Yet not only was he resistant; the Israelites did not want freedom; they were comfortable in their bondage. Life might not have been that great; but it was familiar. They did not remember the time before slavery so they could not comprehend anything different.

"You are being called by Creation herself and sent by the Star Seed people to free humanity from the bondage of separation. They do not know anything else, so they aren't interested. They feel quite justified in their anger, fear, and rage; they know only separation and most of them have never been able to consider what Oneness might be like or even if it could be possible.

"Being possible isn't a blip on their radar because it hasn't been considered. The people, most of them are living in such depths of despair – and don't even know it. Most of them have no concept of a life fulfilled; they only long for a bit less suffering.

"You are sent; you and others like you are being born on the planet to open pathways of consciousness. You might not open awareness of every individual you encounter but you are opening the possibility; creating pathways for those who are open to even consider and then see a possibility of something different.

"It is a total game-changer for humanity on earth. We did not know how it would work or if it could work. But we have seen and know that your journey is impactful. Will it change completely in your lifetime? Perhaps not, but the possibilities are filling the wavelength.

"Soon, one day, these wavelengths will become not only a path through the jungle of humanity, but eventually as more people discover them, they will become paved roads, and ultimately expressways.

"It is happening, and it is happening now. Look at the messes — look at the disturbances that have been underground for so long; look as they pop up to the surface.

"The poison of separation by which humanity is drugged is being diffused by each person awakening. By each moment of Oneness, by each millisecond of possibility.

"There is more light available to planet Earth than ever before. And it is the expanse of light that is causing the visibility of more darkness. In years past, darkness covered the earth; the darkness of separation; of loneliness; of fighting and competing — there was no other way to survive the muck the planet had become.

"Now, as there is increasing light, we see the darkness, the evil, the ignorance that has been underground for so long. That is a good thing, even though it seems not enough. It may appear to be not happening, but it is. It is happening right here and right now.

"We are so grateful for you as you stepped up to your role even though you did not know what it was; but instinctually you recognized and you knew there was more to life than fighting fear, than fighting violence and anger; than fighting anything.

"You instinctually realize that love is the way; that silence and spaciousness is the key to discovering that love. You know. We appreciate you for that.

"You have passed through initiation after initiation; you have continued to say Yes to each mission; you have realized us in your dreams and yet you have felt alone. From now on, though, we will be with you always – in consciousness and in conscious awareness.

"The time is now; the next stage of unfoldment is fast upon us. Until now, you have succeeded beyond our expectations and you are released from your role. However, if you choose to continue, we would be most happy."

••• 4 •••

Randall

SHERO LEFT THE wise woman Ulima's garden and returned to the beach. It was almost uncanny that no one was around; no one approached her. She could feel them hiding but not visible to her physical eye. They were as if sitting on pins and needles, wondering what her answer would be; what the next phase of the journey and the path would be.

She walked into the waters and let herself be basked and bathed in the shimmering, glimmering waters. This time she was cleansed and emptied and then filled again. Filled again with a resolution, with a knowing of the work that was to come before her. She was in alignment and she was supported in ways she had not recognized before. Randall, the dolphin, appeared again, vowing support, remembering, and wisdom, along with a healthy dose of play that would sustain the harder days.

She would find a place to live on the ocean side and commune with the dolphin on a regular basis. She would stand for healthy waters, for cleaning the ocean bottoms; she would stand for the vision she had received and gather like-minded people along her side. Not all would be on the awakening path, but they would be taking a stand for something.

Social injustice, the climate, the earth; and more. The common bond would be the gathering attraction; then the work would begin. She would be in the ranks and an underlying power; an underlying current of "there's more here. Let's start here and then let's do this work." She could feel the children arriving to parents who were ready. Some more than others. Some consciously; others who would be triggered by those children.

The dolphin celebrated her newfound awareness and her newest mission by dancing and spinning and jumping his joy! "Come for a ride," he called to her. She jumped on his back and flew. Flew over the waters, under the waters, shimmering along, glimmering along, each moment. She became one with the dolphin; one with the waters and one with the being she was becoming. She was one with her mission and One with all that is.

Randall returned her to the beach line where Michale once more awaited her. There was yet another celebration meal in place. No one asked her about her decision, for she still had the sleeping hours before she was called to make her announcement, but the air was alive with possibilities. The birds were singing, the animals gathering, and the mood was celebratory.

That night Shero slept soundly. There was nothing, no dreams, no vision, no traveling. Simply sleep, like a baby. It was restful and complete. It was as if there were nothing to do or think or say or create. It was a moment in time that was tranquil and restorative. At first light, she planned to get back to the beach but decided instead to go straight to wise woman's garden.

Of course, Ulima was waiting for her with a beautiful delicious breakfast. The garden appeared even more gorgeous that morning than the day before. Ulima rose and greeted her with another one of those cosmic, embracive hugs that Shero was coming to know her for.

In the embrace came the questions. "What have you decided, my dear one?"

Shero sat and replied, "I accept the mission. I am the one we've been waiting for. For this I was created and for this I am to be. What do I need to do now? I'm ready to begin."

"Allow this moment to sink in; eat and enjoy the beauty of this breakfast," Ulima said. "Then we celebrate. For now, we join forces and we see, we call into being, the possibility, one potential, one presence of your new journey.

"I'm sure you have additional questions. I'm sure you will want to embrace the gifts of this community before you go."

Ulima continued, "From this moment on there will be intention in each moment; intention in each action and each word. There is a coming together of the village of Star Seed, just as when you were created and planted; they all called you into being. They all called you into your present form. We do that again, and yet this time, you will know us always. We will be a team; become Oneness with you in all that you take on. Feast now, my child. Feast now!"

They ate in blissful enjoyment of each morsel of food. They ate with love and appreciation of the moment, of each bite. The party was just getting started.

Ulima called the village together in the center where it all began only a few short days earlier. The villagers came within minutes, gathering in anticipation of a great and grand announcement that would change everything.

Wise One Woman called for attention and introduced Shero as having decided and ready to announce her decision. Whichever way she decided, Ulima said, we loved her, we honored her, we celebrated each moment of her being right up until this moment. The villagers waited with anticipation, holding their breath.

Shero took the center position and stood there. She took time to look around at the villagers, most of whom she had not yet met or spoken to directly yet feeling their love. She was loving them, taking time to gaze at each person. Then she looked at Wise One Woman and said, "I have come to a decision. Although I know it was mine to make freely, it was not really a decision; it was only realization.

"I am one with you. I am Star Seed. I am home and I have accepted the mission to return to Earth and take the next step in the journey. I will return to take a stand for our beloved planet and the souls who live there. I stand for Oneness, awakening, and for the brilliance of potential to be unleashed. I stand for the end of separation and the realization of Oneness, of love. And I humbly request your assistance. I ask and call upon each of you to take a stand with me, to offer your support and your resources as we enter a new dimension, as we lead the world into new and uplifted ways of being.

"I know it will not be easy; I know it will be dangerous at best; yet I know it is mine to do.

"Will you stand with me?"

The chorus of "YES!" was overwhelming; the applause deafening as the entire village chimed in together: "This is for what we are created. You are the One and we are the Ones."

With that, Shero found herself once more in her own space; lying on her bed. She awoke, returned from her journey inspired, filled and in awe at what was being revealed. She had spent three full days on Star Seed Planet and yet in Earth time it had only been an hour. She checked the alarm she had set and saw it was set to go off in a few minutes. She smiled with gratitude and appreciation for the ability to time-travel and return at precisely the right moment.

As she stood and stretched, she contemplated all that had occurred in her experience. She marveled at the journey and knew in some strange way that the timing was exquisite and something very surprising was about to occur in her life.

···5···
Who am I?

WHEN SHERO HAD entered college, she hoped for a new life. She went as far away as possible from her Midwest hometown, eager to escape the oppression of not fitting in and not being recognized for who she was rather than who her family wanted her to be. She wanted to find herself and her people. She went to San Diego, mostly to be close to the beach, and she found herself enthralled with the courses in human-rights advocacy and activism.

Shero knew she was different and wondered if she would ever meet someone like her. She thought with a cosmic worldview that was uncommon in her hometown. She studied incessantly. By now she had overcome the intense shyness of her younger years and was constantly reaching out to strangers with her natural and innate ability to connect with them. She didn't know what she was doing, she only knew that connecting with strangers was easy for her and she felt both comforted and empowered by helping them somehow.

She had hundreds of acquaintances, but very few friends who knew her heart. In her first year of college she had a roommate named Jill who, while she didn't quite understand Shero, accepted her for exactly who she was and how she was. The two young women became inseparable. They became the family they had both longed for in childhood.

Jill was service-oriented too; she loved jumping into any cause that was front and center and organizing a movement for them. The movement could be as small as providing a meal for a homeless person or a ride to someone who needed it. She thrived on helping others.

Together they became known in college as "the revolutionaries," those who would not only step in and help in any situation, but who would and could organize an entire student body on a moment's notice. They ultimately were put in charge of organizing the student body, which in those years became known for their assistance; for their political and personal social activism. They stood for justice. They stood for Oneness; they stood for equality for all people no matter what color their skin was, who they loved, or what they worshipped. They loved people and in turn helped to impact a student body that also loved all their students.

Over the course of their four years at San Diego State University, crime went down, disturbances virtually disappeared, groups came together for all kinds of reasons. There was a general sense of community, of love, of acceptance, that grew across the campus; that flew across the campus.

The teachers on campus were quietly astounded. They did not quite understand what was happening and chocked it up to a general change in culture. In secret they wondered if these two eccentric young women had something more to do with it or if it was something else.

One time, there was a disturbance in the student bookstore. A young man who was a relatively new student was picking on the cashier; he was loud and obnoxious. The campus had become so peaceful that this disturbance was out of the ordinary and caused quite a ruckus.

By chance, Jill and Shero were walking by the bookstore at this time and happened upon the noise. They looked at each other and without words chose to enter the store.

Jill went in one direction and Shero in another. Shero approached the young man directly and asked him a question. He was so wound up he was startled by the simplicity of the question. He turned on her with malevolence and spat at her, "Who do you think you are, asking me that?"

She replied, "I was just wondering. How can I serve you today?"

"What does that even mean?" he demanded.

She looked at him with eyes of love and compassion. "It appears there is a problem here that you are involved in and I was simply wondering if I could help you."

"Why would you do that?" he barked.

"Why wouldn't I?" she replied.

At the other end of the store Jill was holding space. They did not have words for it; it was something that came naturally to each of them and together they had developed an unspoken code.

Jill was standing a few aisles away with her hands open, eyes half-closed and seeing love. She was seeing love coming from Shero into this young man and noticing that he was unable to receive it. She was softening the energy around him and creating a spaciousness that wasn't there moments before.

She kept her hands open and did the work that came to her from that place she could not describe.

Shero continued to gaze at the young man herself. "What do you need?" she asked gently.

Suddenly, he broke down and began to look away, tears glistening in his eyes. "No one has ever asked me that," he said softly. He dropped the persona of tough guy, became more leery than aggressive and she stepped closer to him. "What do you need?"

"I need nothing!" he barked.

Shero responded, "Why don't you come with me; let's go have a cup of coffee."

"Okay," he said reluctantly and apprehensively. Off they went.

That was a normal occurrence for Shero and Jill but the crowd in the bookstore was stunned. They gathered around thinking, what just happened? What transpired here? What do those girls have that the rest of us don't?

Shero and Jill became the talk of the campus. What do they have? Why do things like this happen when they arrive?

Meanwhile Shero, Jill and the boy – who was named Bill – went to the coffee shop and talked for hours. While initially still barbed and cautious, Bill began to soften and relax. In the course of casual conversation, the three became instant friends. Shero and Jill had never had that happen before – when someone they had helped became a friend. Over time Bill melted into the love he experienced with Shero and Jill. He wanted to know everything about who they were and what they did that caused him a complete turnaround with a single question.

At the coffee shop, Shero asked him again, "Bill, what do you need?"

He responded, "I don't even know how to answer that; I don't know what that even means."

Shero gazed into his eyes with the magic that only she seemed to hold and asked deeply, quietly, almost without words, "What do you need?"

Bill responded, almost without knowing what he was saying, "I need to be seen, to be recognized. I fight my way all the time because if I don't, I shrink and disappear. No one notices me; no one says hello and here you are a stranger asking me the only question I could hear."

Bill was a tough guy; he was large and solid. He had been kicked off the football team that morning and was reacting to losing not only the opportunity to stay on the team, but also potentially his scholarship and everything he'd worked so hard to get. He came from a rough background and was terrified in that moment that he would have to return home and would never, ever, escape the horrors that lay there.

He felt seen and heard and accepted by the two girls in a way he never had before; not on the football team and certainly not at home. They were able to talk for hours about anything and nothing. Bill quickly became a tag-along; wherever the two girls were, he was with them.

••• 6 •••
Introducing the Invisible

ONE DAY THE three inseparable friends were talking about the synchronicities that seem to happen when they were together; the mysteries and the adventures they experienced. Out of the blue, Bill asked Shero, "How do you know? How do you know where to be or who to talk to? I never see it coming, yet you are always there in the middle of something."

She replied, "I don't know, really. I just get still and then it appears; the words, the actions, the connection. I get quiet every morning and listen. I was so lost as a child that I began early on asking the invisible to guide me, to lead me. And it does, and it has. The invisible seems to have so much more awareness than our human selves."

"The 'invisible,' what's that?"

"Tell us more," Jill chimed in. "I want to know, too! I know that when we are together, when Shero is around, magic seems to happen. When we walk into a room like we did at the bookstore the day we met you, Bill, things seem to slow down, open up, and miracles appear. I don't understand it, but I know I love watching it and being a part of it."

"Teach us!" they both exclaimed.

Shero had never considered teaching before; she had never considered sharing what she considered to be her private life, but it seemed time. She said, "I only do what comes, but why don't we try it together? Let's sit in the silence together and see what happens."

Until then, Shero had never told anyone of her journeys to the unknown; had never mentioned her quiet time to anyone, much less what happens to her and how it sustains her. She began to invite Bill and Jill in. She began to lead them into the silence to see what might happen. From there she began to talk about her experiences; to teach them what she knew.

The first time, that day in the living room, Shero said, "Okay, let's sit together. Close your eyes and take a breath in."

Bill nor Jill had ever heard of meditation before.

"Simply quiet your mind, then empty it. Bring your awareness from your thoughts to your body and notice what you notice. Noticing is not thinking, but rather becoming aware outside of your thoughts . . . .

"Imagine looking down, down, down into your beingness until you reach a still point; it is like a portal in the center of your being. Look there, draw your awareness there. Then go through it. Let the door of that portal open and enter the other side."

After sitting in the silence for a few minutes, Shero said quietly, "Begin again to focus on your breath. Feel your feet and your fingers. And when you're ready, open your eyes."

"Holy cow!" said Bill. "What was that? This is where you hang out? Let's do it again!"

Shero said, "Wait a minute; hold on, let's talk about what we experienced first."

Jill began to relate her experience. "The door opened, and I found myself at the very edge of creation. It was vast and dark but lit up at the same time. It was at the edge of the universe as we know it. Behind me were the stars and planets; the Milky Way. I could sense the sun and moon and even planet Earth, but I was no longer on it. In front of me was the cosmos. It felt like infinite possibility. It was spacious, yet unformed. It felt expansive; infinitely free, and yet filled with possibilities.

"The weirdest thing," Jill continued, "was that I didn't know anything about any of this and it was at the same time familiar."

Bill jumped in to share his experience, "I saw the Earth, like being up above it. It looked like a beautiful blue marble. It was surrounded by the planets and the sun and the moon. I saw its role in a greater universe – we, Earth, are not alone; we are part of a much bigger picture. I saw and felt that the problems we think we have, are only slight blips on a screen of eternity."

Bill was stunned, not just from the experience, but also with the words that flew out of his mouth. He had never spoken like that; never had an experience like that; it blew his mind. Everything felt different to him.

"What about you?" they both said together.

Shero responded. "I travel almost every morning before I get out of bed. Sometimes I journey during my dreams, but consciously I reach down into the portal each day and connect. For me, it is as important as eating and moving my body. It is like it fills me; breathes life into me and gives me both the courage and strength to go forth each day.

"I've never shared this with any one and I was concerned about doing it. But now after hearing you, I'm feeling like we should do this together often. What do you think?"

Wholeheartedly, they agreed. They exclaimed, in similar words: "It was wonderful, I feel so different. I'm stunned. There are no words." Shero sat back in her chair and witnessed her friends as a deep inner smile came across her being.

That began a weekly ritual. While other college students were out partying on Friday nights, Shero, Bill, and Jill were having their own adventures. They would journey and then talk about what they experienced. They shared openly and with a curiosity that further inspired their journeys.

Bill began researching meditation and Jill began looking at other esoteric practices. They talked about what they were learning and how they could use it to better themselves and humanity. It became a calling for the three of them to explore and impact the lives of the people around them.

···7···

Betrayal

BILL AND JILL became Shero's closest friends; they were her family of choice while in college. These were the two that were her kin, her rock, her people, the ones on whom she relied. They knew her heart, saw her for who she was and who she was becoming.

They were a force unto themselves; inseparable – until they were no longer. One day there was a break in their energy field. Over time Jill and Bill fell in love and began to close out Shero; they started hanging out together, without her. They started having secrets and adventures on their own. At first Shero loved that they were falling in love; then she began to feel jealous. She started feeling abandoned; left out; even betrayed. As she began feeling these feelings the thoughts that were beneath them became a toxin within her.

She had never in her life felt like this. She had never ever experienced even the inklings of that which would become jealousy. It was foreign, and most uncomfortable.

The betrayal came later, just after graduation, when suddenly, the threesome was no longer. Shero broke contact with Bill and Jill and found herself alone. Alone in her own life, Shero expected to go on without a blip; telling herself she didn't need them anyway; that they had been college friends and that phase was now complete. Yet, her emotions floored her. They stunned her with their intensity. Even though Shero was the one to make the break, the feeling of betrayal crept in alongside the jealousy. Jealous, abandoned, betrayed. It made no sense, yet the combination of those emotions caused a break in her spirit.

She had a memory of being abandoned as a younger child but couldn't quite bring it up – it was vague and did not make sense to her. Her family was still there; they did not understand her or her way of being, her life choices or who she was, but they were always there, unconditionally accepting if not understanding. She could not put a finger on the memory, so she blocked it out.

PART 2

••• 8 •••

The Lion

IT WAS DARK, it was cold, there was a feeling of dampness in the air and in her bones. She felt a fear that was paralyzing. She was not quite aware; her cognizance not quite there. As Shero returned to consciousness, she realized she had been knocked out. As she regained awareness, it came slowly. She looked around and found herself in the bottom of a shaft – like a well, deep and narrow.

How did she get there? What was she doing there and now what? These questions began to arise, not with an urgency to answer, but rather like slow molasses creeping around in her head. She had been running, but from what? Glimpses of two worlds float through her awareness.

There was a lion; she was being chased. But there was something beneath that; it was stirring in her. The deeper, dark secret she'd spent her life avoiding. It was beginning to seep into her and she pushed it down deeper. She wasn't going there, not now; hopefully not anytime soon; maybe never. It was a secret she kept so deeply she didn't even realize she was carrying it. Turning quickly from that crack in consciousness, she looked back to the material world. Why was she here? What had happened?

Her memory was spotty at best. She was between worlds; drifting in and out of consciousness. Drifting between worlds; paradoxically. The mists of oneness floated in and around the shadow of separation; the sense of peace wrapped inside a fear of being found out. Was she aligned with who she was or was she a fraud – teaching all things spiritual, but not really believing them? There was a gap between the reality of the outer world and the deep inner knowing she thought she had. The chasm had been getting so big she couldn't hide from it any longer. She was about to be found out; her cover was crashing around her and it left her vulnerable in a way she promised herself she'd never feel again. Where did that promise come from, she almost wondered as the thought drifted away.

Down she went again, into the blackness of the unconscious; passed out again.

Yet once again, she opened her eyes – had it been minutes or hours? – she wasn't clear. This time though she looked around with a deeper sense of reality, whatever that even meant.

She became aware of her physical surroundings. She was indeed at the bottom of a long, dark shaft. It was cold and dank. She had fallen, but how? The memory came, she had been running at full speed when she had tripped and fell. Down and down and down. She recalled a scene from *Alice's Adventures in Wonderland*; when Alice went through the rabbit hole. As she sat up, she scanned her body. Nothing appeared broken or sprained, although there was a big knot on her head.

She was alone and afraid; cold and trembling. What just happened? she thought. She pondered her circumstance, wondering how she was going to survive this. How did she get here? What was she running from and why did she fall?

A memory began to return; there had been a lion chasing her when she stumbled and fell down, down, down this shaft where it now appeared there was no way out.

The good news, if there was any, was that the lion that had been chasing her was too big to get down the shaft. Looking up to see if there was light, she saw that same lion, his head covering the opening; looking down at her. The fear increased as she scampered back along the wall as if to get farther away.

She looked back up at the lion and heard "game well played" in her head. What? She wondered if that knock on her head had caused a screw to come loose. She shook her head and looked up again. This time she looked right into the lion's eyes and was surprised by the love she sensed.

Love – wait, what? Things were definitely not adding up. This lion had just been chasing her; she had been running for her life. She was sure she was dead and not only dead, but the lion's next meal.

I must still be dreaming, Shero thought, as she wondered if she was on one of her journeys. She became curious. Looking up once more, from the relative safety of the shaft, it was as if a secret passed between them. The girl and the lion. It was all a game; it was all creation and it was all love.

The ground beneath her feet rumbled as if in agreement and she burst out crying. The lion, however, appeared to be laughing. His eyes were bright; his huge mane was ruffling in the wind. There was a twinkle in his eyes now.

Shero's crying turned to laughter, a deep belly laugh that caught her off guard. What is happening to me? she wondered again.

As if in answer to her unspoken question the lion spoke. "It's all illusion, my dear, do you remember? You are here to manifest the glory of Oneness; to teach and awaken the world to a new way of being, but you must forget to remember. I'm here to support your remembering. We are all One. It's a game that led to this moment of Oneness." A realization washed over her as he continued speaking: "It's all a game; it's an illusion that keeps us separate. We are all players in a great game called life on planet Earth. You have nothing to fear, my dear.

"In this opening to our Oneness, another layer is unraveled; you will be changed at depth. Now you are awarded a gift, Oneness with all living things, or at least Oneness with all large cats in this jungle, in this moment." He laughed and laughed again.

Looking into his eyes again, she teared up. "Why, oh why have I been so afraid? It could have been so much easier!"

"Yes," the lion agreed, "but you would not have had the experience and adventure and integration that you have now. Look and see." Shero closed her outer eyes and began to turn on her internal sight. It had recently been lost to her but came back in full color now. She saw the path of Humanity and the forgetfulness of it. She saw, as if watching on a movie screen, the evolution of creation through humanity's eyes.

She was curious and watched as a story began to play itself out. It was a story she was familiar with, but this time it had added nuances she'd not seen before.

The story unfolded...

In the beginning of all time when there was nothing and no-thing-ness, yet there came an impulse so great that out of darkness came light. The light was distinguished from darkness and the idea of day and night arose. The impulse of creation settled for a time and then began to grow again. In the next impulse arising from dark and light, there came matter. The matter formed first as a Universe and then many Universes filled with stars and planets. In the many, came an awareness of one planet in particular. On this planet called Earth there came Life. First as a single-celled organism; then plants, then animals, and eventually, humanity was birthed from yet another impulse so great.

In the beginning Humanity was One with all that is, knowing its Oneness, and all was well. It was to be known in later millennia as the time of the Garden of Eden.

Yet, even within Humanity, the very impulse of creation continued: the impulse to evolve; to experience and grow. Since Humanity was One with all that was, a game was created. This game was of forgetting and remembering.

At first, it was an exciting game. Individualized aspects of Humanity took form and forgot that they were part of a greater whole, to have an experience and adventure in human experience. In the forgetting, over time there came a sense of separation; belief in me versus you; I'm better than you, which then led to competition. The forgetting became so deeply instilled that they could not remember life was a game; that they were One. In order to remember they had to forget; in order to forget, the illusion had to be solid.

Over time, as the game continued, more and more individualized particles of Humanity jumped into it; the rules were forgotten. The intention of the game being a game of remembering was lost; buried under a sense of competition and survival.

Fast forwarding to the current time, Humanity had so fully believed in the illusion that was crafted for the game to take place, that they became lost and at risk of destroying their beloved planet. But there was a simple solution.

Looking forward along the timeline, not too far in the future, there appeared two paths. One led to destruction, fear, rage, and the dissolution of the planet.

The other led to a remembering; a reconciliation with love and Oneness. Shero saw a distinct choice point, if only there were enough of the individualized humans who would choose it.

She saw further in the future, a beautiful possibility. One world; One people. She saw the possibility of dismantling not the entire world, but the illusion of separation and therefore the dissolution of anger, rage, fear, competition, hate, and despair. She saw the building of bridges and tearing down of walls. She saw a world of love, compassion and Oneness. She saw the Earth herself reveling in a new saturation of love – Her energies settling down and all beings living in harmony; working together for a greater good.

Shero had sensed she had a role to play in this choice; but now, in her vision, she realized that each time she chose love she was helping humanity to choose love also. She saw in new ways that it wasn't about getting rid of what wasn't working, but rather accepting it, allowing the fullness and choosing anew. In her vision, as she gazed upon the pathway to Oneness, she saw a world awakening, a release of the bullying that had been in place for eons.

She saw a beautiful journey to Oneness; one that although it might take time would lead to such beauty. Beauty of hearts and souls; beauty on the planet and a recognition of Oneness with all that is. Then she saw the realization of Earth being only one individualized particle of Creation and that awareness led to a quantum leap of possibilities.

And then the doubt crept in again. She felt the spiral grabbing her attention, I've done this before, how many times do I have to awaken to the truth of my calling? It feels déjà vu-ish. She argued with the doubt: "Okay, I've got it this time. There is something here that is bigger than me – what's with the lion showing up anyway? – and that wasn't in my dreams. He was as real as I am. Oh, am I even real? Is this real?"

In that moment, Shero looked back up at the Lion with curiosity. She remembered what her purpose was. But why and how did she get herself down in the bottom of this deep, long shaft?

••• 9 •••
Remembering

SHERO THOUGHT BACK, struggling to recall. She was living and working in Thailand. Before she was fleeing from that lion, she'd been staying in a village at the edge of a jungle; where the lion was king. She had been afraid, but of what? She was fleeing; even before the lion began chasing her, she was running away.

The memories were coming, but slowly.

A thought popped into her head, as if something outside of herself was speaking to her.

"Do you see that it was your fear that caused your resistance that caused you to flee? Can you see that running from the King of the Jungle was a metaphor for your life? Where else do you fear? What else do you fear? Where else do you stand in opposition to and in resistance to life itself?"

Shero looked up again at the lion. She was now gently weeping. Gazing deeply into the lion's eyes, the weeping turned into relief and she giggled. The giggle turned into laughter that burst out from her in a surrender that continued to move through her entire being. The lion's gaze dissolved barriers, beliefs, and patterns like a sweltering summer day melts ice cubes.

With each passing moment her defenses fell away; her mind was unraveling quickly. It felt like her DNA was being restrung. All the fear she had carried was dissolving and dismantling. The purity of love and grace in the lion's eyes was pouring into her, loud and clear. It was a warm golden honey feeling, moving through the top of her head and into her veins; from her veins into the cells of her being.

Surrendering into the moment even further, she crumpled onto the ground. She fell into a heaping ball of laughter and tears; filled with that purity of love; filled with a grace that had escaped her until now. Filled with something that had no word and no thought.

She lay there at the bottom of that shaft, utterly spent, empty and full at the same time. How long she was there was a mystery. She must have dozed off, for when she opened her eyes, she didn't remember closing them and looked up again. It was dusk, and dark was quickly approaching, yet the lion remained. It was as if he were keeping watch over her.

Shero came to awareness and realized her paradoxical state. Even as she was in a state of blissful surrender, she was still at the bottom of a shaft with no apparent way up and nowhere to go. She was stuck.

The fear reappeared; it came over her like the dusk over daylight, and it brought darkness. A dark moonless night. She was alone, stuck and afraid again. There was nothing to do but surrender. Nothing to do but wait out a potentially long night ahead. She had very little food and water, and no help in sight. She started to panic.

Then she looked up again. The lion was there keeping watch, keeping her safe, even in the dark of the night. She could sense him more than she could see him. How ironic, she thought, how can this wild beast who was chasing me for so long be at such peace? How can the very thing I'm terrified of be bringing me peace?

Yet, it was peace that she leaned into. As she did, her fear dropped away. She was quiet, not only with her voice, but in her mind and soul. She was safe. She trusted in the moment so deeply that her body, mind, and spirit relaxed deeply.

Shero slept, a deep, restful, dreamless sleep. She slept like a baby in its mother's embrace. She slept off all the remnants of fight, resistance, and running. She'd been running for so long and hard that she was utterly exhausted. She slept until the first morning-sun's rays made their way into the deep shaft.

Shero woke up free, rested and unafraid. She woke slowly at first; remembering where she was, remembering the long chase, falling down and down and down. She checked to see if she might be dead.

No, I'm pretty sure I'm alive, but how? She checked again for injuries, broken bones, strained muscles. Nothing was broken; everything felt good. Scanning her physical body and finding nothing out of sorts, she began to remember the lion and the love. She scanned her consciousness, her feeling nature, her thinking nature. It was there, only love. The love that passes all understanding; the love that washes away all fear; the love that pierces the terror and fills from within.

In this body memory, she scanned again. What had happened? How had she gotten here? What now? She pondered about the love, the lion, and the game to which he referred. She remembered the vision. Now she wondered how the game would end. What she was going to be asked to Be and do from here? She was sure it was big and would push her beyond her comfort zone, but in what ways? What now?

••• 10 •••
Shero's Role

AS AN EARTH-BOUND being, Shero had wondered what her role was. She closed her eyes and slipped back into the vision to watch. *She became an eagle, looking on the moment from far above with eyes that could see all things. She flew down into the vision and looked at her own life. From that moment forward, what might come? How could she choose again? How could she, one single woman, impact an entire planet? She watched and saw another layer being revealed.*

This planet she was on, planet Earth, was being tested. It was time for a quantum shift; but just as with each quantum leap of humanity, there came a choice point. As one species or experience came to a critical mass, it either must change or end. There comes a critical moment in time where a species would either evolve or destroy itself. Either way, it was okay in the view of Creation. Shero saw how Humanity on Earth was fast approaching its own critical mass. The possibility of destroying themselves was likely — but so was a quantum leap.

Destroying themselves was likely because of the amount of fear, anger, and rage; the current life experiences of "me vs them;" the power struggles; the wars; the hatred; the disrespect of the earth as seen in the weather patterns and storms; the disregard of the beautiful blue marble ball of a planet that is called Earth. Earth was rebelling, with the impulse to change getting greater every year. The Earth as she saw it was being poisoned by humans: thrusting chemicals and trash in the waters; cutting down forests; exhibiting a basic and blatant disregard for life of and on the planet.

Earth as an entity was in her own inner battle. She was rebelling and fighting for her own life; with volcanoes and earthquakes; hurricanes and tsunamis; fires and other natural destruction and changes in climate.

Humans and humanity could either quantum leap or not; Earth could either quantum leap or not — regardless of what Humanity chose.

Shero saw the deeper path; the way to choose. It was to release all that was unlike love; it was to choose for a greater good; to lay aside individual desires for a greater collective one. It was to lay down personality and to work together. She saw pockets of good happening, but was it enough? She saw pockets of hatred and power-hungry leaders digging deep below the surface and poisoning the minds of their followers. And she saw many, many people beginning to stand up against the destruction; the separation for something else. But was it enough?

She flew deeper into that now moment and saw how every choice tipped the balance. She saw there was a mighty work to do, but it had to be done in love; for doing the same work in anger or fear tipped the balance toward more anger and fear. She saw that meeting the shadows and bringing them into the light was one pathway. She saw that "fighting against" did less good than "taking a stand for."

She saw that her current situation was a choice point for her own soul, for her work in the world. She saw that as much as she was awake and aware there were things she hadn't seen yet; places she hadn't been yet and that her own growth and evolution was as important as anything else; for it was in her own awakening process that she could serve the world.

The eagle that Shero became and the journey she'd just been on came to an end. Once more, Shero found herself at the bottom of a long, dark shaft and thought, "On a practical level, soon, I'll need food and water. I'll need to find a way out of here and back into my life. Bur first, a few more moments of basking – remembering and reliving the story."

Shero was her name and she'd been called to a village to do something, because of something; she racked her brain trying to recall as her memory returned, thought by thought.

She was in Thailand and had been working for a global agency, as a human-potential activist in various villages for more than a year. She had been brought to that village to heal the judgment that had gotten out of control and was running rampant among the village people.

That judgment was causing all kinds of unwanted outcomes – fighting, stealing, worry, accusations, and a fear that was unfamiliar to the village people.

They had called for help and she had arrived.

Shero was a naturalist, one who studied the nature of people and the world. This village was filled with beautiful and lovely people, but they had caught a virus of judgment and it was running rampant, permeating the village and triggering a fear like no other.

At first, when Shero arrived she had no judgment and no fear. She had seen many things and was able to do her job without hooking into the emotional states of the people she served.

The judgment in this village was different. It was contagious. Moments after arriving, Shero caught a glimpse of the virus of judgment and the fear it was causing. This level of fear and terror were unfamiliar to her, for she'd lived in a world of mostly peace, beauty, and cooperation.

That assignment had been like no others. She quickly came to see that indeed the village was panic-stricken with judgment and the contagion was spreading quicker than a poison-ivy outbreak.

As soon as one person felt judgment and scratched the itch of it; as soon as one person let the fear into their consciousness, it spread. The itch got scratched and boom! it spread. From one idea to another; from one person to another, it spread from child to adult and adult to child. It even spread to the typically docile family animals.

It was that, the judgment, that Shero had been called in to heal. She taught non-judgment, kindness, and compassion. She was well known for her teaching that love and fear could not co-exist. She was the expert in resolving conflict and encouraging peace.

Shero came to the village quite sure she could fix the epidemic by reminding villagers that non-judgment was the way to love, that to release their judgments they would return to peace. She guided people through the judgment maze into nonjudgment, using compassion. It was then that the fear could begin to dissipate that love could be realized and in that love fear dissolved.

She'd been in other villages, supporting residents in overcoming fear and judgment by and with love many times. She was confident. She was clear she was the one for the job and that she could do it quickly.

Then, in less than two weeks after arriving in that village, she was also infected by this very strange flavor of judgment.

It came over her like a poison in her bloodstream that then spread through her body, mind, and spirit. She began to question herself, wondering if she'd been too arrogant in thinking she had the answers and could make a difference. She had in the past; she'd been successful. She was confident going in and then suddenly, much less so.

The first inkling had been when she was speaking with a young boy; a boy who appeared to be very connected to Spirit, one who was loved and revered as a star student in the village.

Being raised to be the next Wise One, he had suddenly turned – terrorized – possessed with judgment. And it was coming out in anger. He had been so kind and considerate to everyone; he was the one who understood love like no other in the village. Then suddenly, he was angry and vicious. Meanness spewed from him like fire from a dragon.

Even as he spoke and the venom gushed, he covered his mouth in disgust and disbelief. He could not believe what was coming out of his mouth and he was as terrorized by his inability to stop it as were those who found themselves targets in his line of fire.

Shero sat with him as together they tried to understand. She asked questions, she held space and she witnessed – to no avail. Then his poison reached out and spewed at her. She ducked but it got her. Right between the eyes. She felt the poison enter her system. She fought it. She denied it. She resisted it, yet she was powerless to it. She too, was infected.

Within hours the peace and calm she had known for years was gone, replaced with at first a slight irritation and mild frustration. As she noticed her judgment and her resistance; it was as if she was possessed. Every tool she had used in the past was immediately inaccessible. She not only couldn't find access to her tools; she could hardly remember having them.

••• 11 •••
Fraud

SHERO'S ENTIRE LIFE work of teaching love and releasing fear was crumbling around her. She began to doubt herself. She began to call herself a fraud. She realized that in fact, she had no idea how to access love in the depths of this judgment that was overtaking her.

In the past she had questioned her gifts and ability to see beyond the realities, to see beyond what was happening in the world, but it hadn't been this close in a long time. It was as if the remnants of her distant past were rising from the dead and rushing back into her consciousness. What if it was all a farce, she wondered? What if she really had no idea about any of it and that the entire light-worker path was false? What if they found out she was only faking it and that she really had no idea? What if they discovered she was really an imposter, that love was a sham? What might happen in the world then?

She worried and fretted. Shero questioned her ability, her calling and her very being as the poison took over her consciousness. The fears began to swirl around in Shero's mind, and she went down a deep spiral of doubt. It filled her veins. She was afraid as never before. She was afraid to leave her hut. She became afraid of the young boy she was trying to help; she was afraid of the other villagers. The fear and doubt grew in her, fast and furious. She could feel the poison running through her system on all levels; physically, through her body; emotionally, she was frozen with doubt; mentally, she was in a spiral that was tight and getting tighter. She didn't understand. She thought she'd been immune to it and here she found herself now filled with shame.

The shame was even more crippling than the doubt and fear. She judged herself and her life with criticism that shocked her even more.

Weeks went by without her leaving her hut except for food and water and the poison was only getting worse. It was growing daily within Shero and it continued to spread through the villagers. Soon they were all infected. Shero lost all awareness of being a healer; of being one who knew; she forgot who she was and what she was there to do. She was drowning.

The shame that overcame Shero sent her into a depression that locked her in a prison within her poisoned mind.

The overcoming darkness swept over her so deeply she could hardly breathe. She had lost faith and had very little energy. She was embarrassed and isolated; she didn't speak to anyone. She was alone and a failure; afraid and humiliated. Disgraced, her thoughts became all about her – what were others saying? She'd let them down, then even forgot to care. She forgot about everyone else as she struggled in the depths of despair.

Then one day, she looked again at the villagers and saw their pain. The shame surged within her, almost overtaking her consciousness, especially when she looked again and saw the suffering to which she'd become blind. She looked again and saw misery upon misery. It was dark and heavy; it was too much to bear. She obviously was not helping and realized that she was, in fact, part of the problem.

It was then that she decided to leave; to run away. She was only another burden here, a failure. It was time to go; to leave with her head down in shame. As hard as it was, as shamed and scared as she was; she made a decision. At first light she would disappear. No one would notice and no one would care.

She packed a small bag with a change of clothes and a few food items and left. She walked out of the village in a new direction, worried about running into anyone and having to explain where she was going. She snuck off without saying good-bye to anyone. She walked a few hours without incident, her predicament blinding her sight. The sun was high in the sky, but her spirits were in the dungeon.

She was unaware of her surroundings; she merely kept walking in desperation and despair. Suddenly, she felt a presence – the hair on her arms raised in alarm. She froze as a different kind of terror flew over her body. Frightened as she was, she stood frozen in place for a moment, then slowly looked behind her at a lion that had appeared in the road. He came slowly, taunting her, as if to say, "I'm here – I've got you for lunch – what are you going to do about that?"

Frozen in place, she dug deep and found only more fear. She was rooted to the ground. She realized that she was so not ready to be the lion's lunch. As miserable as she was, she had a clear thought, "Fight or flight is better than frozen. In this case I have no fight against this lion, so flight is my only choice."

She ran as fast as she could. She ran and ran and ran. Her mind was blank, her legs burned, the pain matched only by the burning in her lungs. She could hardly breathe. She could hardly pick up her feet, yet she continued. Looking back over her shoulder, she could see the lion galloping at an easy gait, right behind her. There was another thought, "Oh, come on and get it over with," when suddenly she tripped and fell, and fell, and fell; down into the very shaft she'd found herself in that morning.

As she remembered, she wondered, "Where's the poison? Where's the fear?" It was gone. Then she recalled the love in the lion's eyes, the humor and amusement as she lay there at the bottom of the shaft and the love and compassion that followed.

Shero marveled again at the lion. She marveled at herself as she recalled her own emotion; the fear and the laughter. Once more she scanned her being. This time not only for physical harm, but also for the emotional and mental aspects.

She scanned for the poison that had infected her veins and the very cells of her being. It was not there; not a trace of it. There was only unadulterated love. A pure presence of being – like, but unlike love she'd known before. It was as if it had been quantum-fied.

It was coal turned to diamonds. It was diffused light become transparent and translucent. It was warmth and sun; it was a cloudless day after an overcast season.

This love was unlike any she'd known before. It was closer to the love she'd been teaching about yet didn't even know was possible. She realized she hadn't known that she didn't know love until that moment.

Shero basked in the love and let it move through her being. She opened her being in unfamiliar places and let it flow. She remembered again the lion's persona; wondering what the lesson was; wondering who the lion really was. She looked up and there he was.

This time she connected deeply to her own heart and spoke from it to the lion's heart. "Who are you?"

"I am your greatest fears personified in the form of the king of the jungle; massive in size and strength – known to eat critters like you for lunch," he bellowed.

"Then why didn't you?" she asked.

"Oh, that would have ended the game with little reward or success – there was a greater game at hand."

"What might that be?"

The lion replied, "For all time, we've had this arrangement. I'm here for you; never against you. I'm to show up as your greatest fear in critical moments to help you remember. To help you graduate to a new level. Your teaching is right-on and not new; you will embody it even more fully. Now you can begin to understand at deeper layers what you've been teaching so brilliantly.

"Feel it – does it feel the same? No, of course not. You've moved to a new level; you've lived in and through fear like never before and you landed in a new dimension. It was your willingness to see me that opened the doorway, that removed the veil of unknowing; revealing a new love.

"Congratulations! Job well done, my good and faithful friend."

As Shero gazed up at the lion, she began to recognize the truth of his words. At that she began to recognize him as her beloved true and tried companion, in new form. The love between them flowed, pure and unfiltered. Unadulterated. It flowed and grew and flowed and grew and flowed some more. She was once again washed in a beauty and grace she'd never experienced.

Rested, at peace, in amazement for the experience and in deep gratitude, she wept again. In these tears, residue of anything and everything unlike love washed over and off her.

She entered into deep compassion for her own journey. Forgiving, blessing, giving thanks for the village, the poison and even her own ability to be freed of it. She felt benevolence; she felt a magnanimity; profoundly moved for all she'd experienced.

She was awake, enlightened, and blessed. She was at One with all that was and all that is. Up she looked again to the lion. He was beaming; his job was done as well. He knew in his heart that his role with Shero was complete;

that he had pushed her into the awareness that was his to do. That his presence was the exact thing necessary for the quantum leap in Shero's life.

Shero looked again at where she was, at the bottom of a shaft that was long and deep; narrow and steep. What was she to do now, she wondered with amazement; with longing and yet aware there was no anxiety or fear consuming her awareness? She became curious; in wonderment like a child. "What's next? I wonder how I'll get out of this place?"

••• 12 •••
The Village

AT THAT MOMENT, as she looked around, she discovered a glimmer of light in a space behind her. As she gazed at the light and became curious, the light began to grow brighter. She approached it and explored it with her hands. What she discovered was an opening. As she placed her hands into it, it was as if the light grew even brighter; a doorway formed, leading to a tunnel. As she bent down to enter the tunnel she was flooded with a deep sense of well-being. She continued in and through the tunnel with confidence yet was in no hurry. When she came to a corner, it appeared to be a dead end, yet with absolute trust and security, she pushed against the wall and it fell away.

Shero found herself at an opening with a slight rise. Looking up she saw blue skies, the edge of a forest, and what appeared to be a beach. She climbed up and out of the tunnel and slid her feet into the warm sand. She had made it. Yet another journey; yet another adventure, and she was whole again.

Shero knew in her heart it was time to return to the village; to do the work that was hers to do there. She was blessed beyond measure to have gone through the darkness, the judgment and fear; for now she embodied love more deeply.

Shero made her way along the beach following her intuition; following the brilliance that now appeared to be within her; her very own shining star. Suddenly, a path appeared. As she walked along it, she wondered again without the previous anxiety she had felt: how would the village accept her now? Would she be allowed back in? Would they be angry with her? Certainly, they would be judging her, but would they be able to see past their pain?

She arrived at the village in the late afternoon. The people did not offer a warm welcome. They were leery of her. She had been so filled with judgment and had become so mean; they did not trust her. They were filled with anger and fear, not trusting anyone, for the poison that spread through the village was all-encompassing.

Yet, Shero's light shone brightly. She called the villagers to the center. They approached with reluctance and apprehension. The people gathered around her as she spoke of love, as she radiated and beamed love to all people. She was no longer afraid, her doubt disappeared as she approached each person with love.

Not with words but with love radiating from her heart to theirs, she witnessed each person, seeing their pain, struggle, and knowing that their inner light, although dim, was still there.

She asked the village for forgiveness; from young child to elder; to please forgive her transgressions, her own anger and fear. She asked forgiveness for her inability to heal or help them and for her inadvertent contribution to the poison.

She blessed them with such gratitude and love that her light was palpable. The young man, the boy who had first infected Shero, came to her and asked forgiveness. This initiated an opening; the villagers began to listen, although still wary, they were a bit more receptive.

By dark, in the light of the full moon, which had suddenly appeared, Shero told the story of the lion; of her plan to run away without saying good-bye; her feelings of failure, of letting them down and of her own fear. She told of her desire to help and how stunned she was when she herself became infected by the poison of judgment and how that judgment triggered in her guilt and shame and how it incapacitated her ability to help, to move and even to think clearly.

The village people listened skeptically. Yet as Shero continued speaking, they began to soften. The hardness in their eyes began to be replaced with a curiosity; the tenseness in their body language began to loosen. Over the hours something miraculous happened; not just to a couple of them, but to many of them, from the babies to the elders.

The first sign of a shift was when toddlers who had been hanging behind their mothers' backs came into the center of the circle and began to laugh and dance and play together. That hadn't happened in months. Then the smallest of babies quit fussing and began cooing and babbling. The elders could feel their bodies, yet remained reluctant to trust their new feelings right away. As they became willing, though, they could feel the change in their bodies before their minds.

The young men had the hardest time. There was too much attachment to the poison of judgment, which led to blaming and protecting themselves with more judgment and fear. Eventually, though, they were willing to witness the others, which gave them space to consider, to become curious and in that opening the love began to sneak into them.

As Shero continued talking she was offering an energetic and quantum-healing presence. It was that energy that began to move in and through the circle. She began to ask questions, to engage the people in sharing their experiences of the past months. What did they notice in themselves and in the village? She created a conversation that was magical, because it was not about words. It created an active space that allowed love to flow. That was the reason they had brought Shero to their village in the first place.

As the night deepened the villagers came to a nonverbal agreement to return to their huts and continue the conversation in the morning. They thanked Shero for returning and for the spaciousness they were beginning to feel. The love would become as infectious as the poison had been.

The softening, the conversations, and the healing continued over the next few days and weeks. As the love became palpable the fear fell away like shackles being removed; judgment became compassion.

As Shero returned to her hut that night, she reflected upon the past few weeks. She had come to the village to transcend judgment and fear into love and compassion. She quickly had become infected and was unable to help anyone, including herself. That produced such shame and guilt that she fled. Yet it was in the running that she came to a deeper integration of her own shadows. She realized she could not heal that which she had not experienced. Her return to the village, once again, served her and her capacity to help others. She became once more washed over with gratitude and appreciation for all she had experienced.

And that was the beginning of the next chapter of Shero's life. She was called to be a healer; she was called to be a spiritual teacher; and never again would she be afraid of being a fraud or allow herself to be plagued in self-doubt.

··· 13 ···
Born Different

GROWING UP, SHERO had never been a normal everyday type of girl. As a young child, she knew she was different from those around her, yet she felt as if no one could see her; that she didn't belong. She was extremely shy and would hide behind her mother's back. She was a beautiful child who was gifted and smart; everyone liked her, much more than she liked anyone. Even as a toddler she had special eyes; they were a bright azure blue and were luminous when she was happy. They turned a darker shade of blue when she was shy or afraid. Although there were many people who loved her dearly, and she had many acquaintances, she did not have close friends.

She was born to loving and kind parents who had married young. Her dad was 20 and her mom was only 18. They had desperately wanted a child since they were first married. When they became pregnant seven long years later, they were over the moon with happiness. They lived in a small farm town in the Midwest, very close to where they had been raised themselves. The town was typical in that everybody knew each other and considered everyone family. Their happiness was not overshadowed when her mother had a series of dreams. The dreams indicated that their baby would be otherworldly and that she would be called Shero. Her mother brushed the dreams off as nerves in having a baby, but the idea for her name stayed with her.

As a baby, Shero would gaze at the ceiling or into the corners of the room. Her eyes would glaze over, and she would coo and smile at the nothingness. As she grew into a toddler, she was quiet and withdrawn, already much preferring to be by herself than with others.

When she was a teenager, Shero would lie in bed at night and wonder what in the world was wrong with her? What was her problem? She simply did not relate to the kids around her or even to her family. She definitely did not fit in at school. She was interested in so many things cosmic, in consciousness, although she had no words for it. There was no school for it. Her few friends thought she was weird and wondered why she couldn't just be normal like they were. Why did she ask so many questions about things no one else even understood?

Her family tried hard to encourage her, to support who she was, but they were at odds with each other about how to do that. She was so different from other children. Her parents often talked in whispers at night, "Who is this child we are raising? Why does she have nothing of us in her? She doesn't think like us; she doesn't even look like us."

They would agree to keep loving her and see what happened. Then another time they would worry, "She's so different, she struggles so. Why won't she try harder to be like us and to fit in? Her life would be so much easier." This was where her parents differed. Her mom wanted to love her and encourage her to fit in, to try harder; to try a craft, or take up a sport. Her dad, on the other hand, wanted her to become even more of who she was, regardless of what others around her thought or did. They argued at night, and Shero could feel it.

There *was* something unusual about her, she knew that. Even as young as she could remember, she didn't belong. Until Shero became a teenager, she had an imaginary friend. He was with her always, especially as she journeyed in her dreams. They were the best of buddies. He was the one who understood her; the one who stood by her when she was so misunderstood by her parents. He was ever-present; with just a thought, he was there. He didn't offer much in words, but his presence was kind, loving, and compassionate and Shero felt safe knowing he was there. She would talk with him, imagine with him, play with him and dream with him. It was as if he led her dreams; he was holding space for her to become all she was here to be. He was there for as long as she could remember – even in the crib, comforting and encouraging her as a newborn infant. She remembers his calling her name at night and playing with her during the day.

Her parents said she had an active imagination, but she knew he was real. She called him Michale and relied on him; he was the only one who understood her, even as a baby. She talked with him, worked her thoughts out with him. He was more real to her than her parents and family. He was her constant companion.

At first her parents tolerated it and chocked him up to an active imagination. But once she entered school, they began to worry. They began to encourage subtly and not so subtly to put the imaginary friend away or at least only to bring him out at night when she was alone.

Because she wanted so to fit in, she began relegating Michale to her bedroom and to times when they were alone. She continued to rely on him and would even disappear into her room during the day so they could be together. Michale was her best friend and he was a wonderful listener. But he didn't say much. He didn't answer her questions really, he turned them back to her – asking, "What do you think? It doesn't matter so much about what I believe, but what about you?"

When she wondered, "What's wrong with me? Why am I so different?" Michale would respond, "You are exactly as you are and that is perfect for me. You are brilliant; you have a purpose on the planet and one day you will know what it is." He was masterful at making her feel better but really didn't give her much information.

She wondered why she had never noticed that before. She guessed it was because she did feel better in his presence, in his arms.

Then one day he disappeared.

When Shero was younger, her parents had admonished her about her imaginary friend. They thought her friend was causing Shero to be different. They told her she needed to live in the world and put childish things away. At that point, she quit talking about her friend, she quit speaking about her dreams and journeys. She even quit asking as many questions as she had in the past. She withdrew into herself even more.

Then one day when she was 15, Michale had disappeared. It was frightening; it felt like abandonment; it was betrayal at its worst. She could no longer feel him or sense him around. It was the worst day of her life and there was no one she could talk to about it. She railed, she fought, she wept into the silence of her bed, buried under the covers. "Where are you? Where did you go? What did I do that made you disappear?" It was the saddest time of her life. She was alone.

She wept for weeks because Michale would no longer appear to her when she called him. She mentioned it only one time to her mother who promptly responded, "Oh, thank God he's gone, now you can get along with living life in the real world!"

She mentioned it one time to her dad and he said, "I'm sure he's still there, just no longer visible to you now that you are older. It is not appropriate for a girl your age to spend so much time with an imaginary friend. Perhaps now you can make new friends, girls your own age who you will like."

Neither of those answers made her feel better. But over time, she adjusted; she decided on an unconscious level that if Michale weren't here with her anymore then she was really on her own. She was going to make the most of it and never need anyone again.

If Michale could abandon her, she thought, then she best forget all about him, too. She relegated him to memories of being a young child with an active imagination. She forgot all about Michele and his promise to be with her always.

••• 14 •••
Inner Drive

AS A YOUNG adult in her mid-twenties, things were going fairly well in Shero's life. She had found a way to function in the world in a way that was somewhat satisfactory. She had discovered a path in which she could be real; in which she could speak her truth and teach a few people what she was learning. She began her work as a human-potential activist, which allowed her to travel to remote places in Thailand and South America. In her heart of hearts, she knew this was her calling, but it had gotten a bit stale. She was saying the same thing to the same people every week and they were not changing. She wondered if she was really making a difference. She yearned for spiritual adventure. She yearned for a deeper experience of that which she was teaching.

At heart, Shero was a loner. She loved go to a beach and commune with the sand, the waves, the wind, and herself. It was at the beach that she felt most at home; at home in her body and in herself. It was the beach that brought her solace in times of grief; comfort in times of uncertainty; strength when she was tired; and clarity when she was confused.

Shero did not feel as though she belonged on this planet. She felt as if she had been dropped into the wrong skin, into the wrong life. From an early age she had dreams that took her places she almost recognized – but not quite. They were beyond her life and always helped her to feel connected to something greater than her life and body. When she was young, about six-years-old, she had her first journey, the first that she could remember as a dream. She had been crying and her parents had been exasperated with her. She was talking about her friend and they kept telling her she had to let go of her imaginary friend. As she fought the ideas her parents were presenting, she fell into a deep sleep.

She journeyed from her bedroom into a forest. It was a safe forest; one filled with trees and lush groundcover. She was not afraid, but instead welcomed the newness. In this forest she made friends; friends with the deer and rabbits; she made friends with a raccoon she named Mask. She and her friends enjoyed each other; they would play and frolic in the forest; run down to the stream, take turns splashing in the bubbling brook and laugh and laugh and laugh. These animals were her friends; she was safe in her skin in this forest.

In the forest there was always a surprise; something new and different; a token; an idea, an experience to which she could return. These became her favorite moments. Shero learned very early on not to talk about her dreams.

Her parents had been frightened about the active imagination Shero displayed from a very young age. They worried about her and constantly reminded her to live in the world; not in her imagination.

As she matured, Shero was called to be a naturalist with a focus on studying humanity. She became learned, but most of what she discovered, she knew innately. Shero was committed to the betterment of humanity. She listened with ears beyond the physical; she saw with an invisible eye into the hearts and souls of those she was working with.

Her life was dedicated to the awakening, but she didn't even know what that meant.

From early childhood, she had an inner drive that her parents didn't understand.

PART 3

••• 15 •••
Journeys

SHERO HAD ALWAYS had vivid dreams, or at least that was what she called them. Really, they were more like shamanic journeys. She would fall into a deep sleep, almost trance-like, and journey out into the worlds beyond. As a child she learned very quickly not to talk about those types of dreams. They were not welcome nor understood and they always caused her parents to whisper and worry about her.

She'd close her eyes and would be taken to a land far away; to a land of dragons and creatures unlike any she had ever experienced. Sometimes the journeys would be explicit in detail, with a very clear adventure or experience. Other times the details would be vague, and she would return with a general sense of wonder, connection, or inspiration. Although she could and occasionally would initiate a journey, there were more times when she was simply taken out without warning and without a conscious plan.

One evening, Shero sat down and without a moment's thought found herself standing in a deep and narrow mountain valley; it felt ancient, not of modern or current times. The sun was setting, and dusk was fast approaching. Shero recognized this as a journey the moment she looked up and saw an orange sky peppered with magenta. It was beautiful and eerie; nothing like anything she had seen in her waking hours.

She realized she was back on a hero's journey; one she'd found herself on many times since her childhood. Even as she realized this, she was overtaken by the veracity of her senses in this strange place.

Shero finds herself in a place of no time or space; between worlds. She's been here before, but this time she's so freaking scared she can't think; she can't move. Frozen in fear is such a weak statement; this was so much more. This is the "frozen" of all time. This is frozen in thought, in action, and in being. The very blood in her veins is frozen. Nothing is moving, nothing can even breathe – even her breath is frozen. She is petrified.

Think of the petrified wood we see and cherish – there is nothing in this that she wants to cherish, being frozen in time, frozen in space. She doesn't even know exactly what happened to cause the freeze. The deep freeze. The freeze of the very cells of her being. Even her thoughts are frozen.

Frozen in time, time is frozen itself. She fears she is about to be lost forever in the deep freeze, frozen moment. "Okay, breathe," she tells herself. Something beyond her conscious mind responds quietly, "No, not yet, feel how it feels to be frozen solid.

Feel how it feels to be frozen in time and space. Notice the stillness, the void, the nothingness. Now feel the fear; the very fear that caused everything to stop. Notice it from below, looking up at it. Notice it from above, looking down into it. Now begin to breathe into the freeze."

Breathe and breathe and breathe. No breath yet, only frozen particles of being. She can feel it; the particles trying to break free enough to be breathed.

Locked in no time and no space, she begins to relax into the terror, into the frozen — there is nothing else — no thought, no emotions, only the freeze. She becomes the terror; she begins to become the freeze. She has a thought, "What if I stay like this forever and forever? I can't even imagine moving beyond it. I can't even imagine how to take the next breath, much less the next step in my being."

And then there is another thought: "Frozen in time; oh, it's not so bad. I'm still here." Beginning to separate a bit from the experience, Shero observes herself frozen in time and space. Not moving, not breathing, not blinking. She becomes the observer first of herself, then of the situation in which she has found herself.

What she observed increased her terror and caused her to freeze even further.

There was a huge, ugly dragon heading straight for her. Shero trembled with anticipation. Even as her mind kept her frozen in place, her palms got sweaty; her heart rate picked up and she could feel her blood pressure skyrocket. She could feel the strange sensation of being frozen, yet a cold sweat was running down her back and her brow, trickling into her eyes.

That fear surprised her; she had not been a fearful person. She had been called courageous for most of her adult life. The things she'd done without thought stunned some people, especially her family.

The places she'd gone, the risks she'd been willing to take; but nothing, nothing at all had prepared her for this moment.

Frozen in fear; alone and afraid. Keep breathing. Notice the breath, notice the abundance of the moment. It is stretched beyond time and space.

Shero noticed the spaciousness between her breathing. She noticed what she noticed. That her hands were gripped, that her feet and legs were tensed ready to jump into action, yet frozen in place. She noticed how her eyes were frozen. Then, that they began to move ever so slightly.

Her sight was coming back into alignment. There was something here; Shero moved to non-focus so she could sense it. She already knew she wouldn't be able to see it with her physical sight; it was deeper, higher, just hidden from her conscious awareness. It was this thing that caused her fear and terror.

"What is it? What is there? What lurks just beyond my consciousness?" she wondered. She didn't try to figure it out; she surrendered to it; surrendered to the process; surrendered to the experience. If she'd learned anything at all on this adventure called awakening, it was to not make up any story about anything she was experiencing. It was to let the process unfold as it would. She did not try to control it. She did not even try to understand it; that would come later in the safety of her home after she'd completed the journey.

Shero opened to surrender, opened to receive. What is here? What is next? What is it this time?

The form inside of Shero began to take shape. The form was a monster of sorts, big and dark and scary, very much like that dragon who was flying toward her. The underlying energy behind the image was "Be careful or you will be dead." Be careful of what you do, what you say, who you are, or you will be sent to the ends of time. Those who are in charge do not like these truths you are speaking; you are giving people too much power and presence. It is not going to be allowed. You will be scared to death. Meaning you will die, and it will be the fear that kills you.

Letting, allowing, surrendering into the image, Shero kept breathing. She noticed her feet and hands. She noticed the space in which her body was and the image before her.

Shero knew in her bones this was illusion; that is was a process, a dragon along her journey. She chose to face it straight on, not in fight or flight, but in curiosity – even in her terror, even in her frozen state as her consciousness was taking charge. The inner dragon and the outer dragon merged into one – one flying toward her at the speed of light.

Looking, seeing, telling the truth; what is this thing? Looking deeper beneath the big scary dragon, she began to sense the underlying belief. She still believed that what others think about her made any difference in her life – to her at all. She sensed the bigness of this fear, she'd dealt with it many times before, yet this was the biggest, most terrifying dragon of all.

Shero continued to focus on her breathing. Her breath was returning to a normal rhythm, the ice particles melting with each breath. Yes, her breath was returning – but her body was still frozen in place.

Facing the inner dragon, facing her deepest fear, her biggest challenge up to this point, she surrendered. In surrender she remembered the truth. "There is nothing and no-thing against me. This, too, is for me. This, too, is for my awakening, for my hero's journey. This, too, is for my becoming."

She began to breathe a bit easier. She still didn't know if she'd get out alive, but somehow that didn't matter as much. If this was her time, she'd be ready. She knew it was all a big game this lifetime and that there will be more to living beyond the physical.

In some ways she was ready to drop the struggle, the constant challenge, the constant dragons.

In some ways she felt complete; yet even in her desire to be done she realized it was not time. There was one more challenge to overcome. There was one more place to face, one more opportunity to fully realize her best-ness.

She faced the dragon. She watched it. She breathed with it, she began to feel again, the blood in her veins thawing a bit and beginning to flow. The shock of this thing, this terror, was beginning to release. The fear was still there but now alongside it was the presence of curiosity. What was being in her consciousness now?

She continued breathing, returning to her body, returning awareness to her body slowly, rhythmically. From her feet – feel your feet on the ground. Feel the ground beneath your feet. Feel your toes; they are gripping. Relax the toes.

Shero stayed alert and consciously relaxed. She moved her awareness up her legs, knees, hips. She felt her breath begin to unfreeze them. She relaxed her muscles; relaxed the terror. Moving into her hips, buttocks, and belly. She noticed what she was noticing, feeling her physical body first. Back to the body. She removed her mind from her body. Removed the fear from her body. She breathed into her belly, ribcage, and chest. She felt her shoulder blades; felt her arms from the shoulders to the tips of her fingers. She gently flexed her hands, relaxed them, opened the fists she had unconsciously formed. Opening, breathing. No thinking; only feeling her body once again; she was separating her mind from her body and her body from the emotions of fear.

Shero moved her awareness up the column of her neck, over the occipital bones, over her skull; moving across her forehead, she began to become aware of her eyeballs in the sockets, her jawline; and then relaxed her face. Fully back in her body, she had the ability to notice more clearly what was happening around her.

She noticed that her mind was still frozen in fear but that it no longer had a hold on her. She raised her awareness yet again and came into the truth of her being; the truth that was love and only love.

"What if love was here, what would I notice?" She became curious once again about the image, the dragon, that loomed in front of her.

As the observer of herself, Shero watched. She observed the nothing-ness of the moment, the nothing-ness of being.

Then thoughts begin to arrive. She wondered, "How can I be frozen in fear; what is happening in me? What is happening outside of me; what is happening?" Yes, her thoughts were frozen, yet beginning to thaw around the edges.

Her breath began to move, just a little, like water under a frozen surface. It began to break off like pieces of ice from the frozen mass. It was slow and laborious; one breath at a time.

With her breath came an awareness of that which is greater than she. She remembered she was safe; she was always in the Creator's hands. She was protected at her soul's level. That didn't mean her physical body was always safe; it did mean she'd said yes to this adventure of becoming and she knew there would be obstacles along the way. Even in the journey, even in the unknown, her soul and being were safe.

Shero's attention was once more drawn to the dragon, who was now right in front of her. She could climb, she could cower; she could run, but why? Instead she took a deep breath and calmed her nerves. She took another deep breath and connected to her body, attempting to bypass the fear running through her emotions and the frantic thoughts in her mind.

The dragon roared; fire was coming out of his mouth, his breath putrid and hot, like a wind blowing past her. Close enough to see the flames; close enough to feel the heat; the hot heavy, smelly stream. Knocking her back a few steps; it was nasty. The dragon was huge and could eat her in a single bite, if he so chose. She should run. She should wake up from the dream; but she'd had enough experience to know that dragons bring a gift, if she was willing to stand there long enough to receive it.

Shero felt the terror. Her mind was saying run, get out of there or you will die! But she resisted her mind; she chose instead to feel the terror and do something different: she chose to walk into her fear instead of running from it.

••• 16 •••
Love in the Face of...
or RUN!

EVERYTHING IN HER being called out, "RUN!" Yet she stood her ground. She put her hands on her hips and shaking in her shoes, bellowed, "What are you? Who are you? Why are you here?"

The dragon stopped short, surprised to be addressed. He roared; fire spewed from his mouth. "Why am I here? I'm here for you to face your deepest demons. I'm the dragon of fear, I am here for you.

"You need to be fearful. You should be scared of me; terrified of the fire coming from me." He began roaring again and again; fire flying every which way.

Shero stood her ground. Feet planted, hands on her hips, even though she wanted to cover her face with her hands and escape the dreadful smell and texture of his vile breath.

"Hello, Dragon of Fear." Shero was quivering in her boots. "Even as I feel fear, I refuse to give into it. I stand my ground and I address you. Standing here with you, not running from you; I see you. I see the show; the outer terrifying show, but I want to see the real you."

The dragon roared, and emitting even more fire. "Who are you to address me? I am the Dragon of Fear!"

"Why are you here?" Shero demanded as she stood her ground; fighting every urge to recoil.

"I'm here to scare the living daylights right out of you. To intimidate you into submission. You stand on the edge of mastering your fear and my first job is to unleash all the hidden fear within you."

"Well, it worked," she said to the dragon, "what else?"

The dragon shifted subtly. "I'm here to empty you of your remaining fear and terror. So many humans live in adjunct terror and subtle fear – this is it. I'm here for you to experience it and to be terrorized. As you stand face to face with me, the oppression of inner fear can be dismantled."

"What do you need?" she asked, "what do I need to do?"

"As you stand here with me, not wavering, you are doing the exact thing that will transcend the fear." He stood, still discharging a few flames. He pondered and eventually said, "I need your love; that is all I need."

Shero took a long slow breath, letting go even further. "I can do that," she said slowly. "You still scare me; I am still fearful that you will burn me with your fiery breath; or eat me; or continue terrorizing me, but I can offer you my love."

The dragon made a strange sound — not a roar, not a bellow, but some sort of strangled snort. Then he laughed out loud and Shero followed suit. Game well played. Checkmate. Success. They continued a conversation about their roles in this play. Shero told him how truly terrified she was, what had happened in her being, in her body, mind, and experience. He laughed again.

Shero said, "That was definitely the most frightening experience I've ever had, and the fear is still with me, but it doesn't have me as prisoner. It's more like a memory."

She knew that she would wake up at home and process through new layers of fear; new layers of terror as a result of this journey. She was willing to do this for the ultimate surrender. She was willing to do this because she knows she's clearing not only for her own awakening, but for all of humanity.

As Shero woke up in her own bed she had a deep realization. "The fear — that fear is the absence of love. I look and see. I journey into the minds and hearts of those terrified daily. My heart breaks in compassion; my heart weeps for the pain and hopelessness of so many on the planet. Now I realize on a new level the depths that fear, and terror can reach. Freed yet again, I recommit to my work. To the healing of the planet.

"I'm here; I stand for the awakening of the planet — the awakening into love, the release of the bondage of fear and anger; of separation and distance, feeling alone and disconnected.

"It's not even disconnected, it's un-connected. The sense of isolation that so many live in – it breaks my heart again and I weep for the enormity of the job ahead of me."

She wept and even as she said the words of recommitment to the task, she wanted to quit. It felt too big, too vast and she wondered if her actions really made a difference. If all her effort would eventually pay off. She was tired.

Even as she wept, though, she realized that this was the work she signed up for; this was the position she agreed to. It wasn't an outer agreement with another that she made, but rather an innate knowing that for this she was created. She did not know of the risks, as there was no fine print. Even as she did not understand it, she knew the job was two-fold: continue in her own awakening and bring that to the world at large.

Shero wailed, "Sometimes the world seems so large, the project seems so unreachable I feel afraid. I lose hope that anything I go through makes a difference. That anything I experience makes a difference to the world."

She wondered about her life; how she was so different from anyone she had ever met. Why does she have these experiences? Why her? And most of all, why does she have to do it alone?

••• 17 •••
Finding Bliss

SHERO HAD AN uncanny ability to see things. She could see a person's emotional and etheric body. She didn't even realize this was not normal; it had been with her always. She could tell when one was fearful or distressed; angry or hurt. She was able to drop her own resistance, her own emotions, to listen with the eyes of her heart. It didn't happen all the time and when it did it was both a gift and a curse. It was one of the reasons Shero stayed away from groups; away from large gatherings of people and why she had only a few real friends. She built a protective wall around herself so she could navigate without being taken out. Sometimes the emotions she walked into were so thick and deep they brought her to her knees. Other times, she felt her energy system being drained and did not know what to do with the emotions that poured into her. Much later, she learned this was called being an empath or a sensitive. In the extreme, a person like that did not recognize their own feelings because they were so fraught with others.

So many of Shero's coping skills were not conscious; she had simply learned to deal with her life to the best of her ability. She wasn't taught what to do with her gifts; how to navigate the world of the invisible; therefore, she became attuned to an inner knowing. It was an inner impulse; one that when she listened and followed, it served her well.

For example, one day Shero could have an impulse to enter an area that on a normal day, she would never had attempted. On another day, she would not go to a common place, one that she frequented often, but the inner knowing, and impulse was no, to not go. For the most part, Shero listened and followed, for in her experience, listening was better than the cosmic 2-by-4 that might appear if she did not.

Shortly after Shero completed her time at the village in Thailand, the one she affectionately called the Lion Village, she traveled to South America. She continued her work in several villages in Colombia and Venezuela. She had taken some time off and was traveling on her own when she found herself at the mouth of a waterfall. She knew instinctively this was a sacred place. She'd been feeling it, had been drawn into the jungle, along a slightly worn path for the past few hours. As she approached the waterfall she fell into silence, feeling awe, wonder, and the unique electricity in the air that indicated something spiritual was about to happen.

She sat on a rock nearby the fall and dropped all thought. She closed her outer eyes and opened her inner eyes. She let go of all the things that had been on her mind; the things she had been contemplating and thinking about. She entered her inner sanctum and opened herself to receive. Shero offered herself to Spirit and to the waterfall. She surrendered anything and everything in her awareness and unconscious in order to be present to this moment. She felt it was an initiation.

In that moment she knew. Shero stood up and carefully entered the water. She found two stones where the water fell into the pond and she stood there, looking up. Placing her hands upward in connection; she stepped right into the falls. The water was frigid, icy cold, a shock to her system. She prayed, "Release from me any and all that no longer serves me; conscious or unconscious. I'm here for You!" She stood there for a few moments, water rushing over her. She felt a deep energetic, cosmic cleansing, like the water was releasing her and the pond and earth below were taking away all the negativity – all that was less than love and light and stripping it from her.

It was exhilarating, exhausting, and exquisite. She was emptied.

Shero stepped back for a moment, looked up with thanksgiving, more awe, and deep gratitude. Then she entered the falls once more. This time she was filled. The water rushing over her was filling her at a cellular level. It was igniting the light, activating joy, and stimulating her soul.

When Shero stepped back she felt on fire with light. The very atoms of her being were vibrating at new levels. She had had the experience of being light-headed before, but this was light-bodied.

She could hardly move for the joy pouring through her; for the bliss she was experiencing. Bliss was permeating, penetrating, and filling the inner spaces of her being. It was exquisite. The edges of her body were dissipating as she merged with the light. As she looked up through the forest, up to the sky and sun, she felt these words: "You are my beloved, in whom I am well pleased." It was a moment that would stay with her forever.

She was initiated, baptized in the Spirit of Light and acknowledged for both who she was and what she was doing.

Shero sat at the edge of the waterfall for hours, basking in the new vibration and frequency of her being. She was One with all of creation. She was One with the falls, the earth, and the sun. She was one with herself. She had come home to her soul once more in a new way. Shero stood and began the walk back out of the jungle, seeing a glimmer on everything. It was as if she were now seeing with her eyes the vibration of everything; the jungle, the leaves on the trees, the bark, the flowers, and the sky.

She walked, amazed, enthralled, and in Oneness with all of life.

She was One. She was in bliss and grounded in her body. She was at peace and in joy at the same moment. Content, fulfilled. At-one-ment.

Shero continued in this state for a few days before she felt the crash coming. She'd experienced it before; after an intense expansion, there was often a letdown. There would be something that shook her out of the experience of expansion, and she would dive into what she called the experience of a denser emotion. She realized this was part of the expansion and contraction process; that each expansion brought more light to her being, and then more density was revealed. Something in her subconscious was being released. It was as if expansion always had a kick-back. But she was not ready for this one. Even as she became aware it was headed her way, she tried to avoid it; she wanted to push it away and bask for much longer, but she could not stop it. She ultimately surrendered to it, threw her hands up and exclaimed, "Okay, here we go! Let's take this ride."

··· 18 ···
Frustrated

SHERO WAS TOTALLY frustrated, frustrated in a way that burned in her soul. Her belly was tied up in knots; she simply did not know how to proceed. Every angle she took turned into a brick wall. Every step had her fighting and banging up against barrier after barrier. It was one of those days that had turned into one of those weeks. She knew she was on a hero's journey and she knew that here would be opportunities and challenges; that there would be dragons and chasms – dragons to kill or face down; chasms to cross, mountains to climb and terrains to leap. She knew it and yet in this moment it did not make it any easier to take. She was fighting that very fact – she simply did not want to take the dive. She wanted to remain in the Oneness she'd found in the waterfall.

It was like Shamanic medicine burning in her belly – the resistance to the frustration alongside the deeper knowing that to go through it would bring relief and healing to her soul. She'd felt this medicine before. The work was to feel the feelings and surrender them to love, but it was hard, and it burned through her. She knew there was a breakthrough close, but she just could not find it. The frustration that burned in her belly was hot like a fire, and she fought against it. She wanted to remain in the bliss state; desperately did not want what was presenting itself. There along with the frustration burning within her, was another frustration – with herself.

She recognized the feeling, the frustration that came when no matter what was going on, she couldn't see the way through, she couldn't feel her way. And beneath the frustration was anger; beneath the anger was something else. What was it? What was going on?

There was nothing in the outer that was happening so what was it?

She had just returned from bliss, from her time at the waterfall. Her heart had been opening wide and large; free and unburdened. Barriers had been coming down like sandcastles. Obstructions had been dismantling like the outgoing tide, taking those sandcastles down; melting them away.

Then this frustration and irritation with everyone and everything showed up. It was burning her up inside; she could feel the flames eating at her. And it was affecting her work in the world. What in the world was going on inside her? What was happening?

As Shero felt into her experience she realized it began with an incident with a colleague named Carmen, who had become Shero's nemesis. While Shero was usually attending to different villages, in the field and working by herself, there were times she was involved with collaborative projects at the global agency. Carmen was not exactly her boss, but she was in charge of the global projects. They'd had history for years of not seeing eye-to-eye. It felt to Shero that Carmen was continually and intentionally disrespectful to her. Shero dreaded those times because she often felt stilted, stopped in her flow, and generally hindered and obstructed by Carmen. To Shero's face, Carmen was cooperative and supportive, but her subtle, just-below-the-surface behavior irked Shero to no end. It was a pattern in their relationship.

She had been on her spiritual journey long enough to recognize a healing in the works. She knew that as soon as she could surrender into the frustration, the deeper issue would be revealed, and she would be freed from it at which time she'd be able to address it with poise and calm. She also knew that the surface issue was only the trigger to a deeper healing within her. Yet, the underlying issue would burn and niggle until she could surrender.

Shero's process was burning through her right along with the wildfires that were burning only a few hundred miles away. Burning deeply within the forest and burning deeply within her. There was a correlation; there was a relatability. But what was the underlying thought? Or did it matter?

She was so incredibly frustrated and irritated – and if she got honest with herself, angry. Angry because she was feeling put aside; not valued, not honored. She had time after time made herself available to others; to Carmen and whatever she needed. Yet the more she accommodated, the worse it got. That day the virtual meeting had already been rescheduled twice and Shero had plans and was eager to get to the village people she was working with. The time was scheduled for 10 a.m.; then Carmen messaged again – there was another issue in her life; she couldn't make it on time, and could we please push it back two more hours? Most of the time if the scheduled allowed for it, that was no problem. But this was a pattern and an inconvenience. Instead of simply saying no; she acquiesced, she bent – the meeting was important, and Carmen's excuse seemed reasonable. Yet, it triggered Shero's anger. She let the anger flow through her. "What is beneath this?" she wondered. Inconsideration; being put off; never being the priority. Wanting to get a job done that simply was extended; now for months. Anger bubbled and frustration brewed. She immediately got a headache and knew she had to clear this anger before she could do anything else.

 The amount of anger seething through Shero over a relatively small thing was an indicator that something else was amiss. Something was out of balance or there was something going on within her that needed attention. As she consciously sat with the anger, she discovered a thread. This thread led her to an awareness of the pattern she was in. The pattern was just under the surface of her consciousness and it had been showing itself in bits and pieces.

 Diving deep, becoming willing to look, see, tell the truth and then take authentic action, Shero settled in. She closed her eyes and looked. "What is going on?" Following the thread, she noticed several occasions where she hadn't spoken up; where she hadn't expressed her truth, but instead swallowed it; not wanting to make an issue over something that wasn't. But she knew better; swallowing things without processing or speaking them always created an issue within her.

She continued looking. She found places recently where she was feeling put-out; not honored, and certainly not respected. Knowing that this was inner work, she looked more deeply.

She saw. There had been a conversation a few weeks ago that didn't go as Shero had hoped. She had been expressing a need to be heard and instead of hearing her, the person on the other side of the conversation tried to fix it and then blew her off. Since Shero had still been in a blissful state from her time at the waterfall she didn't think too much of it, simply returned to her peace. That was the origination, the beginning of this thread. Instead of going back to him and speaking again, she began to internalize it. The beginning trigger of an old story, an old belief that she didn't matter; that no one understood her anyway, was launched.

As she recognized this thread, she identified a pattern of her childhood. As much as she had healed inner wounds and released subconscious patterns, they could still kick up now and again. A point of awareness came to her.

Looking at the pattern of "I'm not understood," she began to see the out-picturing of that pattern as a belief of "I don't matter" which then led to "I won't ask, I won't share." She realized the more she allowed the pattern to surface and she didn't share authentically, the more the feelings got pushed down and then something would happen and boom! – that anger that could have been dealt with as a simple irritation and a useful conversation fired up in her once again.

Shero identified the source of both her current frustration and the thread behind it. She then began to feel it in her body. Where did it live? Where was it burning? She found it in her right upper shoulder, into the side of her neck.

As Shero began breathing with it, giving it space to be; to feel the feeling behind it, both the physical sensation and the emotional ones; she began a conversation with it. She apologized to it for not listening earlier; she asked it what it needed; she felt the fullness of the emotion. The tingles of irritation, the flush of frustration, the burning of anger. She leaned into it, allowing all of the emotional energy to be accepted. Her body burned, tingled, and shook, as she stayed with it without judgment; without trying to settle it. Only after fully expressing it did she begin to soothe it. "Okay, I hear you, I'm listening. What do you need?" she asked the pain.

"I need expression; I need physical release," it responded. "Let's go run," she suggested. "Yes, let's!" the feeling responded.

As Shero ran, she stayed in curiosity, connection, and communication with that pattern and thread; the frustration was willing to be released with a newborn idea, with a new action idea. The running released the pattern. A creativity that came after releasing the anger and frustration was the exact right thing that could move Shero forward.

••• 19 •••
Separation

AS THE FRUSTRATION dissolved, Shero continued in her process to discover the deeper layers of her crash from bliss. She recognized an underlying foundation of humanity. She saw a people who believed themselves to be separated from each other and from God. It was not what they wanted, yet they had created it. It was a people long, long ago who forgot they were one. In their forgetting they made up a new story, a story that had been with humanity for eons. The story was one of separation; it was a story of darkness and in the separation and darkness the people learned to believe in "less-than." The experience of separation produced over time a void within people's hearts. That void came to be filled with all the false beliefs we still see today; the falsities of unworthiness, separation, not being good enough, or loved or worthy. The stories were familiar; humanity still carries them today, thousands of years later. This world is fraught with the assumptions and outcomes of believing in the illusion of separation.

In separation there was fear; with fear, came a fight-for; a distance-from, and competition. In competition there came judgment; a sense of better than and worse than. It was only in separation that one can experience hatred and discrimination. There was a fear of anyone and anything because we don't believe in our worth; we don't believe in our Oneness; competition is the culprit and the outcome.

Shero realized that competition was not the issue; for example, it's not money that is the problem, but beneath money, the problem is greed. In greed comes a hoarding, a protection; a "me against you;" a them against us energy that always leads to fear and more separation. Of course, separation was the cause as well as the result.

It became a chain reaction. In separation came hatred; in separation came violence and thus even more separation.

There came a belief that "if I have you can't have; if you have, I want." It was a toxic cycle that permeated and penetrated the very cells of our being. To Shero, it was not that dissimilar to the poison of judgment the village people in Thailand had experienced.

Shero was aware of this going on within her being and she also knew the antidote to any emotion or attachment to it was surrender. She knew from experience, that surrender was the ultimate letting go of one thing – that which she was fighting – to allow something else; love or connection.

Shero had been around this block before, enough to realize that with most every expansion, especially those that changed her at depth – like her time at the waterfall – there would come a second force. It was like stepping into the river of change then everything unlike the change must come up to be reconciled, surrendered, and processed. She also realized in theory, that letting go and dropping her resistance would make the process faster and quicker. Sometimes it was more challenging than others; sometimes it was easier than other times. Knowing it didn't always make it easier to achieve, however.

···20···
Serve Creation

SURRENDER ALL THINGS that are unlike love or neutral.

She had heard the question inside her meditation, "Are you willing to serve creation?" a few years back. Then with her affirmative answer she was told by Spirit, "Then you'll be asked to surrender everything."

In the beginning when she was experiencing bliss and peace and calm, that seemed like a promising idea. It appeared there was nothing to surrender, as she was love and love embodied.

The first time her heart was blasted open with a laser beam of love it did a total turning inside of itself, so the outer became the inner. Pierre Teilhard de Chardin talked about the "peduncle" in his classic book *The Phenomenon of Man*; that at the end of an expansion there comes a mushroom effect of turning inside out. It was like that for her, where everything turned both into and out from itself. She hit the ground, on her knees in gratitude.

Shero had been to an intensive retreat with the intention of going back into her heart, of freeing her mind to live in her heart. The retreat was facilitated by a man named Charles, who had been her spiritual teacher for a few years. The experience was pure bliss. It was exactly the experience she planned on having but turned out to be nothing like she planned.

In that moment when the universe came down and pierced her heart, the energy of Love filled her being. The barriers to her heart were collapsed and there was nothing but love, pure unadulterated love; it was the pure essence of being and the very source of creation. It was bliss. It was ecstatic; it was expansive.

She thought, "I've arrived. I've come home." She wept with heartfelt amazement, tears of pure joy. And as she wept, she went to the ground in humble appreciation. She was on her knees, not for the first time in her life, but in a new way.

When asked by her teacher to put words on the experience, all she could say was, "Wow … it was profound … it was quiet and full; expansive and pure; it is love. It's as if everything I've been teaching for the past decade has now come into my experience. It's like I am having the experience of my teaching in ways that I didn't even know I wasn't living it."

"I had no idea love was like this.

"I had no idea that creation was this blissful.

"I had no idea bliss could be this sweetness and energized at the same time.

"There were no words; it was mind-blowing; thoughtless and mindless.

"It simply was. I came home to the Universe. I was One with Creation.

"I know my place in the entire Universe.

"It was bliss."

Then her teacher smiled gently and said, "You know you'll be asked to surrender everything."

She replied, "I just did." He laughed with the laugh of a wise elder, and replied, as you might have said to your nine-year-old granddaughter, "Yes, honey, I know you know – and there is so much more."

And there was.

Her inward journey of healing and surrendering was beginning again. There was more pain and suffering to unravel; so much more anger and rage to dismantle; so much guilt and shame to unpack; so much fear and disbelief, doubt, blame and even more than all of that. Shero had a sense she was doing this work not only for herself, but for all of humanity. She knew that each time she entered into a denser emotion and surrendered to it she was helping to free humanity from the prison of separation.

Surrender all that is unlike love or neutral. Surrender. Let go. And the letting go was so ludicrously impossible – until it wasn't.

Shero realized that surrender was the key. She knew it from experience, knew it in her bones. When she had difficulty surrendering, it felt insufferable and unachievable. Many times before, Shero thought she had surrendered at the deepest level and then there was more and then more; and then yet another layer.

Surrender. It became a mantra and daily work, "I surrender. I am willing to surrender; I am willing to be willing to surrender." Some days that was the closest she could get to it. Other days and weeks and months though, she lived surrendered, in the flow and presence of love and grace.

Shero knew that the true experience of surrender was hard to explain until you reach it. It was not being a doormat, denial, or walking away – it was standing in it, (whatever "it" is), until it passed. Standing in the emotion until there came a moment of going through it. "Surrender" was to face it, an emotion or situation; to run toward it when the natural inclination was to run away. The emotions were there, locked in the cells of our being, in the unconscious of humanity – what's in one was in everyone; the microcosm of the macrocosm, a hologram. All people were affected by separation, where these emotions are accumulated if they were not processed. There they hid and remain hidden in the foundation of our being; permeated, penetrated and filling the very inner spaces of our being. If an emotion or experience was in one person of humanity, it was in each of us; both the dense emotions that we call negative and heavy, as well as the lighter, higher ones of Love, appreciation, bliss, gratitude and grace.

The surrendered state, Shero knew, was one of ease and peace and flow. It was feeling the feelings that arise, but not being triggered by them. It was a state of Beingness, and from that inner quiet, doing one's work in the outer world. The outer actions and doing-ness may look the same, but the inner state can be quite different. It is equanimity and from that arises kindness and compassion.

Shero was going along life smoothly when she tripped. Again. She pondered, "So, what happened? What slipped up or got revealed or triggered to start this new layer of processing? What is it now?" There was something burning her up inside.

Shero did not have a propensity to be an angry person; disappointed, maybe; frustrated for sure, but not really angry. She had processed through layers of frustration and anger, surrendering for herself and humanity, and thought she was good to go. Whatever anger she had carried had been released. She was sure of it. Then one day, rage showed up. For no apparent reason with no obvious trigger; it just happened. It just started and boom! there she was, deep in the middle of it and didn't even know what hit her.

The rage burned in and through her like a forest fire consuming acreage. It burned everything and anything in its path. A forest fire can burn for weeks on end; with winds blowing and flames spreading. People are killed, belongings burned. Shero's rage burned through her. It overcame her; possessed her.

The rage Shero was feeling was so intense she realized that she could have killed. She could have struck out and hurt someone in defense. She realized now how people who rampage with guns and mass shootings could do what they do. She realized the depths of anguish that runs when rage is the primary emotion.

As Shero recognized the pattern in herself, she began to see the out-picturing of it in humanity.

The rage that caught Shero by surprise started with a little irritation. It came unaware and grew in her, like the poison of judgment she'd experienced back in the village in Thailand. It was something that she processed and yet could not release or surrender. Each time she went in with the intention of surrendering irritation, she ended up feeling more anger, more frustration; more rage.

It burned for days that turned into weeks that became months. Rage took over her entire being. It was the rage that was hers from years of not addressing or allowing her own anger and the rage of the universe.

Rage for all the women who are #Me-too; who have been victims to men in all manners of speaking. Rage toward the men who perpetrated the victimhood. Rage at those who had betrayed or abandoned her. It was rage at the injustices found in the world.

It was rage at the issues of discrimination; of judgment. Rage was filled with judgment, of someone to her and from her to others. Rage burned inside of her for no apparent reason, and for every reason. The unspoken reasons rose to the surface in waves. Now she saw how rage could be justified. Yet she could not act on it, only feel it.

Shero was burning with rage for the entire of humanity. For those betrayed, for those victimized; for the victims and the perpetrators.

Her rage was burning endlessly. She worked with her teacher, Charles, energetically releasing the core points of rage. Willingly standing in it and surrendering again and again to a greater love. She took on a mantra: "I am processing rage to release it from the cells of my being; from the cells of my being to free myself from its grip; to free myself from its grip on humanity. I process rage for a greater good, for humanity."

Shero could see that rage went back to the beginning of time, when humanity first became separate from the Oneness, from Creation itself. It was a choice, but the consequences were not what was expected. That led to rage. Which led to blaming others; to guilt and to shame. Rage was behind all those emotions. Rage was the fuel for the violence and wars in the world today. If there were no rage, there would be no more war, no more violence.

She looked boldly at today's violence, at the rage that was unaddressed, that was unprocessed.

Then it came to a head.

Shero was at a local bar with her friends on the night of the shooting. They were having an enjoyable time and suddenly out of the blue, they heard gun shots; the shots sounded so very close and were followed immediately by screaming. Screams of pain, of those who had been shot; screams of those close to them; those who were seeing the bleeding; seeing the limbs being shot apart. The madness and mayhem were overwhelming. It was loud, it was surreal; it was excruciating in the reality of it; it was unbearable in the devastation that followed and remained.

Shero and her friends were not physically hurt that night, but many others died, and numerous others were wounded. The shooter was killed, and the community was shaken to its core. Shero jumped immediately into action as she sat with the wounded and dying. She held hands and tried to stop bleeding. Her presence had a calming force, even amid the chaos. She immediately got down to business, being present with one person at a time, as she was guided. Even as the emergency personnel arrived and those who were not injured were escorted out of the building, she remained. She looked into the eyes of many victims that night, reassuring them, sitting with them and holding the space of love. Love over evil; love over violence; love over fear. She kept repeating those words to herself and out loud.

Later, as the last of the wounded were taken by ambulance and the last of the dead were removed, Shero remained. She shifted her attention to the employees who remained. She sat with them, holding space as they processed a full range of emotions, shock, grief, disbelief, despair, and horror. She sat now mostly silent, with those who wept. It was dawn before Shero left.

Days later, Shero was called by city officials. They asked if she would attend a gathering to address the victims and survivors of the shooting. It was said to be the worst and largest mass shooting in history. There had been others in recent months and shootings like it appeared to be more common across the country. The city recognized that the culture that allowed this type of behavior must change; leaders were going to do everything in their power to understand and to change their community into one that was safe again.

Someone had recognized in Shero that night the qualities of one who knows; one who understands. The mayor was insightful enough to include Shero to answer the existential questions; to stand in a place of greater knowing. She was one of many on a panel that included police force and city council members.

The questions came fast and furious. "How can we stand in this? How can we live with what just happened?" The questions were fired at her. The people demanded answers;

they needed answers to put the madness into a format, into a container they could process and move on with their lives.

But there were no real answers. There was nothing that made any sense at all. It appeared to be a random incident, of which there were more and more; Shero felt that was a diagnosis of the country and the world at large.

At the meeting, she pondered the questions. Why did some die, and others were injured? Why did the rest come away unscathed, at least physically, that night? Why were some people there and others not? So many questions and so few answers that made any sense.

The questions continued: What causes a person to be in such pain that they could go into a random place and kill so many people? What is underlying the violence? What can we do to prevent it from happening again? How can we protect each other?

How can you live with it? How can you stop it?

Shero answered as many questions as she could with as much composure and compassion as she could muster. Then she began to ask questions of her own. She invited the people in attendance to consider her questions both on a literal and physical level, but also at a deeper, more personal level.

"How do you contribute to the violence in the world? Where do you perpetrate violence in your own life? How are you the same as the shooter? Where do you live in fear or hopelessness or anger? Are you committed to connection and being in community or are you more committed to being separate? Where do you fear? Where is your anger focused? How do you kill – with your words or thoughts?"

These were challenging questions – the questions people don't want to be asked. Shero sensed that in general people would much rather blame and attack others than look within themselves to find the very things they are blaming.

Before processing her own rage, this event would have sent Shero to the wind and back. But after living and processing her own rage, she understood in a deep, visceral knowing of why and how rage like this can be triggered.

In that moment, the rage that had rocked her for so long lifted, even as she now felt the collective outrage at the shooting. And as she stood in front of the crowd, what was revealed as the rage lifted like a heavy curtain being lifted from a stage, was deep compassion. She had a deep understanding and empathy, not only for the victims; but for the perpetrators. It was from this place that she spoke to the crowd.

"We are at a time in our humanity's history that the violence has to stop. And you/we get to be the ones to stop it. I speak from personal experience. I've been so outraged, so steeped in my rage that I couldn't breathe; that I felt I had the capacity to shoot and kill, but I realized it comes from pain. A deep sense of not being understood, valued, seen or recognized.

"What will lead us forward is for each of us to begin to see each other, to begin to be in conscious community; listening, watching; honoring each person's journey. While I do not condone this person's actions, I do understand how his pain can come to this."

Shero placed the people in small groups so they could share their pain and fear around the shooting. She guided them deeper into the conversations by asking them to share their own pain, anger, and frustration. Innately, she realized that by sharing their stories, they could not help but love each other. The healing had begun.

The gathering came to a close with the commitment of the city and the people to continue these conversations; to continue healing and unpacking what had been hidden and was coming forward for healing.

As Shero worked with the group to process the emotional fallout after the shooting she recalled so many times she'd walked her own journey and she began to realize places within her that had not been fully healed. Places and emotions lingered, like a bit of dust in the corner of a room coming to the surface once more.

••• 21 •••
The First Awakening

SHERO HAD A flashback to a time after college, to the first time she met her teacher, Charles. She'd known for a long time that her life was different from the typical life. When everything fell apart with her friends, Shero took off; she had followed her broken heart from where she was to somewhere else. She had found herself hearing a call that took her to Joshua Tree, California, and stumbled upon a man who saw her heart. He invited her to join a circle the following weekend. In the circle they sat and closed their eyes.

Immediately she was taken from the center of the room to the center of the earth. The journey was fast and unexpected. As she journeyed through the surface of the earth, through the many layers of the planet, she came to the core. At the core of the planet she landed smack dab in the middle of the spiral of Creation.

She was taken to the beginning of time and space where there was nothing; no-thing, no-time, no-space.

It was a void of nothing and no-thing-ness. It was electric with possibilities with no form. She felt the power of the infinite, even as she had no form. Her body had dissolved, her being disappeared even as she was traveling.

She was present when the urge of Creation was so pronounced that from that no-thing-ness came an impulse so great that first it was a dark void and then there was light. That very impulse continued to pulse so that then there were universes and planets, then life itself. Shero felt the very impulse of Creation that created her – her soul and the soul of humanity – from every planet. She was carried along the impulse at each major shift, she felt the leap, the quantum leap from where she was, from where creation was in expression to where it was becoming. She felt her spirit being formed from the quantum field.

She witnessed the creation of the planet Earth, from this vantage point, she saw that nothing mattered.

Nothing matters – that means that all her stories, all her wounding, didn't matter. It was a profound and sacred moment that would change her for all time. Nothing matters. And everything matters.

At that time, Shero came back into her body with a jolt as her consciousness tried to adjust, acclimate, and receive the information she was given. It was jolting and freeing at the same time. As she opened her eyes, she saw the truth. The world was awakening, and love was the path.

From that moment, Shero had taken work as a human-potential activist; traveling the world, primarily working in small villages in remote areas. She had landed upon a truth that was leading her; guiding her and yet was a bit elusive. She had traveled first to Thailand for a few years and then eventually to South America.

She took every opportunity that came, and she went all alone – knowing no one, understanding nothing of the language, yet heeding the call. The call to leave was as strong or stronger as the call to arrive. This was the beginning of her running from herself and the world as she knew it.

Even as she had touched the truth that nothing mattered; she still had a niggling within her. It was as if she had been given a gift but couldn't quite get it unwrapped. She was shown a possibility but did not know how to reach it. Shero was alone as never before. There was an underlying sense of abandonment that would not leave her; the betrayal coursed through her veins, causing her to make vows to never really love another again, to never trust another again, to never open herself to another in ways they could hurt her again.

"Never, ever again" became her mantra. Her focus became the spiritual world and the love, bliss, connection, and wholeness she had tasted with the teacher. She tried to disconnect from physical realms by ignoring her own pain. She went for world adventure. She was still kind and loving; she still had a magic touch with strangers. She magically healed people and situations simply by showing up. She didn't know that was unusual, it was only who she was and who she'd been since forever.

She still did not belong anywhere, she was in the world, but not of it. She knew so much and nothing at all. She stayed busy with others so she wouldn't have to feel her own pain, burying it again and again.

PART 4

••• 22 •••
Role on Planet Earth

ONE EVENING SHERO had a journey that began as a dream. It was vaguely familiar and yet subtly different.

Shero journeyed to a place that felt sacred; one that was only love; one that had no polarity like Earth. There she engaged in a conversation with an elderly ethereal woman who had insights about Earth.

"In the universe itself, there is only love. Planet Earth is one of the places that has polarity, that has experience. However, it has in recently centuries gotten out of equilibrium.

"Earth is no longer a place to go for experience, it is no longer a mastery course in experience, it has become a prison for many of those who live there. The prison of lack, of limitation, the prison of not having the ability to see good, to experience love or to express kindness.

"The wars that are going on have continued beyond what anyone thought was possible. The wars have taken to the streets and are impacting innocent people. Of course, in truth there are no innocent people and no victims and no perpetrators. But in experience, there are plenty of each of those.

"One of your roles, Shero, is to impact the system, to shift the balance of good and evil. To bring light in a way humanity has forgotten. In truth – and ultimately – light will win, but perhaps not in time, before humanity destroys the very planet they say they love.

"The information age, the technological age, has removed people from being in relationship with the Earth. This is killing the planet and the opportunity for such a beautiful mastery school.

"You have been there; you have seen it. Now tell me, what do you notice? What do you find of importance to share with us here?" the elderly woman asked.

Shero thought for a moment before responding. "While Earth is a beautiful planet, it is wrought with challenges. While the people, most of them at least, believe in goodness, there is a poison in their beliefs. They do not believe they are good; they do not believe they are worthy and therefore they fight. Even in love, they fight. Even in kindness there is a competition, a "me vs. them" mindset. They do not see how every action, much less thought, impacts the greater whole.

"They are lost in themselves, not even realizing they are never alone. Not even realizing that the very air they breathe connects them to the planet and to each other."

Shero continued, surprising herself: "At many times, I felt alone, but now I realize I wasn't ever alone. It is the same for *the people there. I want to bring love, to release the burden of their struggle for them to live and love and enjoy this amazing planet they are living on."*

The woman replied, "You do realize what the next step in your mission is? You are to return and to make it your life's work in deeper, greater ways to bring your knowledge into the world.

"You have been doing good, you have been teaching and healing on a small stage, with individuals who come to you and with small groups where you are led. It is time, if you are willing, to go have a greater impact, to take a stand, to make this your stand for all people to awaken to the truth of who they are and who they are becoming.

"It is time for humanity to lay down the fighting, to lay down the violence and realize interconnectedness and justice for all. To see the oneness, the similarities and to gently and subtly teach the 'greater than this one life' awareness. It is time to save the planet for future generations. It is time to turn the tides of violence and destruction back to regeneration and adventure.

"It is time to overturn that which is no longer working and find a new way. You know that way. Even if there are currently no words nor pathways, you know the way.

"We will be sending in new seeds, babies who will have the same life you had. But if you are willing, you will be there to teach them, to guide them. They will not need to be alone as you were. You are paving the way and the way is happening.

"You are the one who will be leading a multitude, a legion of Star Seeds, to restore balance and love to the planet.

"Many hundreds of thousands of humans are waking up, but their percentage is still small.

"There are many who are doing the work of awakening; some who are riding along with the tide and many more who are the resistance. They show up in corporations, in government, they are the poison in the systems. The greedy, the power hungry, the ones who know nothing about the good of all.

"If you choose this mission; you will be called into leadership; you will be called from doing your work in the shadows to being front and center. The light you will receive will not be easy, for there will be resistance by the powers that be. You will be shamed, ridiculed; they will try to stop you in any way they can. It will be even more dangerous than what you've lived through already. And the key is the love; the nonresistance; the key is love itself.

"You are ready, and you will not be alone. There will be many coming, but as babies, so it will be some time before they join you. As babies, those children will begin to disrupt the system in who they are and their incapacity and unwillingness to be systematized. You will see it; you will feel it. Reach out to them and their parents — some of whom will be supportive, and others will not.

"There is an army of light growing, gathering. Will you be the leader of this light army?

"You don't have to answer now but think about it; feel into and let us know what your decision is. If you choose to accept this mission, you will go into an intensive training period; you will meet a teacher who will lead you. If you choose not to accept this mission, you will return to Earth and continue the life you are leading; you will continue as a human doing her work in the world until your natural transition. We will be with you; however, you will forget this experience. You will have a vague memory of a dream, but you will be unable to recall the details of it until a much later time.

"Either way, it is your choice. Either way, you will be honored and appreciated.

"If you choose to end your life early on planet Earth, you will be welcome here, you will be brought here, just as you were today. You will be considered an earth hero – Shero is your name, and all will be well.

"We will continue our efforts and help to assist and transmute the dark energies on planet Earth."

"Why now, do I get to choose?" Shero asked.

"Because you have completed that which you were designed to do. Your role is complete. You can fully retire in peace and live the rest of your days in peace. Or you may choose to continue your work with more conscious awareness of that which is to come and that which is real, even as it is unseen."

Shero first saw the earth as she knew it to be. She saw the ones she had already impacted and the journey she had taken. She saw the village and the Lion; she saw the Dragon and the terror she experienced that froze her.

She saw it all with new eyes, the eyes of the beholder; she could see beyond the reality; beyond that which was, to the greater plan.

She saw her young adulthood, her inabilities and the insecurities she lived with. She saw the ways she was different from her family and now understood why she did not quite fit in. She saw her schooling, the friends she made; the impact she had made. She saw her childhood and the challenges she lived through.

She was able to see the patterns and the invisible threads that ran beneath and over each situation, every moment and beyond. She could see the matrix of her life and her being. She then saw a future projection of one possible outcome if she returned without taking on a future mission.

She could settle down a bit; she could get married to a man of her dreams. She could read and write and simply enjoy the beauties of the planet. She could travel as a tourist and visit all the sacred holy sites. She could do that and be fine. She could be content with that life – sort of. But in looking more closely, she saw an empty place in her tapestry. A place that was while not unhappy, simply not fulfilled. She knew that if she chose to return without taking on the next mission, she could have a happy, quiet, boring life.

There was appeal to that. No more fear, no more challenges, no more lions and tigers and dragons, oh my!

Then she saw a second projection; if she indeed took this mission her ride would continue. The ups and downs, the adventure, the risk, facing all that humanity carried within themselves. It would get potentially dangerous with those who were against the light coming after her in ways that hadn't happened before. She could also see the new Star Seed babies being planted and birthed. They would be little seeds of light who needed a leader. If she did not take on this mission, they would have to find their own way; just as she had.

Although they would not be alone, they would feel like it. The parents and families would ostracize them for being different, struggle with their incapacity to live within the norms of rules and regulations.

They would find each other and band together, creating a new pathway for being. But it would take longer, it would be harder than if she were there to lead, to gather, to be the light. She saw it clearly.

There was no judgment, yet she knew in her bones this was hers to do. She also realized that now she had a new tool, an arsenal of tools, to support her work on the planet. She understood things that had escaped her before.

She was ever grateful for that moment, for the return to the Star Seed planet. She clearly recognized her calling.

Yet she continued to explore, becoming more curious and wondering: what if she did not accept this calling, would someone else? Ultimately, yes, perhaps. What would happen to the planet if she were finished now? Had she done enough?

The visual she experienced was more rage, more violence, more of the apparent destruction that was in motion. She could see the world leaders getting crazier and crazier and instead of standing up against the crazy, the people would hunker down, shudder and shrink. The light would be fought. The people, the light workers, would be extinguished individually and collectively.

The corruptions that were being revealed now would go underground again and take on even more power. The normal people, the typical people, would shrink in terror. They would hide their light for fear of destruction instead of shining it brightly to fight the destruction.

She could see that although the work she had done and planted on the planet Earth was good work, it simply was not enough. She looked again and saw her friends, those who understood her, struggling to understand, fighting the darkness – but not overcoming it.

···23···
New Calling

SHE LOOKED ONCE more; what if she took this mission? What might be one of infinite possibilities? She watched as the planet came to life again, she watched as the planet came to love again. She watched as everyday people, in everyday lives, stood up to the poison; to the darkness and took a stand for love, for grace, for oneness. She watched as ever so slowly the light continued to shine, even in the darkest moments, that more and more people were joining the ranks of light. That more and more people were laying down their swords of anger and rage, for something different, something not yet formed, but for the hope of love, for the hope of Oneness.

She watched as everyday people laid down their defenses and came into nonresistance. She watched as people joined together in compassion for all, kindness for all, Oneness for all of humanity. She watched a people lay down victimization and stand for Wholeness. She watched the movement of light take hold and stand in the face of the darkness.

She watched as this nonresistance stood against terror; she watched as people stood up to being victimized and said collectively, "No more." Then the terror began to crumble. At first it got stronger and more intense, then eventually there was a break in the process — there was one terror that fell, then another. World leaders were exposed and eliminated.

As people stood for each other, the leadership had to fall. They were going to go hard; it wouldn't be easy; in fact, it would be the fight of their lifetime. It would be intense; it would be a battle of wills.

Shero thought of Lucifer and the angel of darkness. It would be a global and galactic war against separation for all time.

And she could be part of it. She could be impactful in a cosmic shift on planet Earth.

Then she looked again and saw her life. She would be stretched, she would continue to awaken in her humanity, she would be standing up against the biggest barriers, up against the waves of hatred, the tsunamis of separation — and she would be forced to stand tall.

She knew she was going to do it; she was going to accept this mission.

And then she went out of conscious awareness and flew with the stars. She went home to the beginning of Creation and even before that. She flew in and through the beginning of time and across the timeline of humanity on Earth from the beginning of the Earth, the planet, through the many stages of illusions. She watched the idea of separation take root in man's mind and heart. Then she flew over current time, seeing the world as it was, and as she continued the flight, she was in the future overlooking the possible outcomes, one potential result of awakening. She flew and flew and flew until she could see a world awakened. A planet Earth restored to beautify and kindness. It was still a planet of lessons and growth; of polarity to have experiences, but the overarching themes were once again love. Once again peace. She saw the darkness receding; she saw the light overtaking it in every corner of the Earth; in every corner of the universe. She saw that this battle on Earth was a battle in the cosmos as well.

This was part of a cosmic shift, part of a cosmic arrow of direction.

She knew in her heart of hearts that this was not the only possibility, but it was one possibility and it was for this she was born. She recognized herself as one who had much more to do.

She saw that creation itself, all of creation was watching to see what would happen on planet Earth. It was the center of the galaxy in this moment and would determine the trajectory of the future of Creation.

In that moment she was clear. In that moment she was humbled. In that moment she was in awe and wonder at why she was the one to witness this. Why was she the one who was seeded? Why her? Why now?

And then she realized it was her destiny. As a woman, as a Star Seed, she was the one prepared to take the next step

Looking further at the evolutionary spiral of Creation into the future, she saw a beautiful world, growing once again in harmony; respect for the planet, for the rivers and oceans, for the mountains and the valleys. She saw a harmony in nature returned to a natural cycle. She saw a people honoring nature

— in all of that which came; the fires; the storms; the volcanoes, the earthquakes. It was all in harmony for a greater good, a greater whole; it was all in perfect order for a greater good and a greater world.

She saw a return of an original goodness, but one with experience. Not exactly returning to the Garden of Eden but entering into paradise after having the experiences of being human. She saw the fulfillment of scriptures of all religions — love, paradise, experiences, and a return to Oneness.

It was beautiful, so beautiful she had tears in her eyes; tears in her heart, and she knew that whatever challenges were going to come her way, she was ready. She was prepared and she would lead the way.

As Shero returned from her journey she knew, somehow, that this awareness would return to her at a later time, but that in the moment the details were already forgotten. She could trust the unknown and would know what she needed to know at the appropriate time. This journey was a gift but was not for her keeping quite yet.

···24···
Forgiveness

SHERO HAD BEEN called to do a work in Ecuador. She traveled from one village to the next, offering human-potential training and assisting the villages to a healthier, more abundant and cooperative existence. Between her assignments, she traveled, free to explore the country and her ever-expanding conscious awareness of humanity, sometimes staying in one place for a few days; other times she landed and stayed for several weeks.

In the depths of a longer stay that became a surrender process on a mountain side, Shero's friends Bill and Jill, came to mind, asking for her forgiveness. She had not thought of them in years. In the moment they arrived in her vision she felt immediately hurt again; immediately betrayed and victimized by the two people she was closest to in the entire world. At the first reaction, the first resistance, she noticed what she noticed and became willing to surrender.

She became willing to look and see. She asked them in: "Please come into my space, let's talk." It was her hurt speaking, but inside it was a willingness to explore. She had surrendered so much over the past months and although it wasn't easy, there was a relief that followed.

As Jill and Bill entered her consciousness, the flood of good memories came first; she really loved these two people. She remembered the first time she and Jill had met and became friends, the work they did in tandem. She recalled the day they met Bill and how incredibly angry he was. They were the ones who helped him release the anger. Shero saw now that the anger she carried was greater than even the anger Bill had at the time.

She continued to notice what she noticed. Then she noticed the pain they caused her. The betrayal, the abandonment, the entire story she had created about those painful times. She felt the deep hurt; the betrayal in the cells of her being.

As she continued to look and see; to feel and release, she then noticed for the first time in a long time how good her two friends were with and for each other; she was amazed she had not seen it before.

She realized that the love they shared, the connection they had, was because of her, in part. She was the one who had encouraged them to explore what was between them. She was the one who saw the love long before they did. She was stunned to see that how quickly, as they discovered their special bond, she forgot that she loved them both. She became the victim, not wanting to be with them.

It was she, not they, who had abandoned the relationships. Years later, she was seeing for the first time the stories she had made up were simply not true.

In an instant, she began willing to surrender yet again – her story, the anger, the hurt, being a victim, the abandonment and betrayal. In an instant of willingness, she saw that she'd made the entire story up. That what she experienced was only her experience. It was not real – they did not have the same experience and in fact their wounding was as deep as hers.

There had been an energetic rift among the trio that appeared irreparable. They each had a missing space in their hearts and minds. They each had a gap in their hearts that was not filled.

And the healing continued.

Shero forgave them both. In doing so, she healed a deep sense of betrayal that she had lived with for as long as she could remember. She was able to see the situation from their eyes and realize the pain they also had in losing her. They had not shut her out as much as Shero had pushed them away. In her own pain, she left them; without even a good-bye. The stories she had made up caused her to leave town without notice and dismiss the friendships she had held so dear without taking any responsibility for her own actions. She'd only held onto her own pain and then buried it deeply. Now, as forgiveness washed over her, she wept.

The forgiveness was a cleansing salve. In her mind's eye; they fell into each other's arms and laughed and wept; they came together again, friends forever; Shero was able for the first time to celebrate the joining of her two besties. They were freed in love, to expand together, not to the exclusion of Shero, but in the wings of her forgiveness.

The forgiveness was palpable; flowing through them like warm honey in their veins.

It was the forgiveness that opened a doorway to a release of the hurt and betrayal and the concept of being a victim. In that moment Shero saw there are no victims in the universe; that was impossible because each person had their role to play. Each person was a set-up for the others in a magical, mystical, miraculous way. She realized that without the abandonment of her friends she would never have experienced the awakening she was currently in. She would never have seen the powerful current between them, and she could never have celebrated the healing.

Feeling alive again, inspired again, she continued exploring the countryside. She could feel an impulse calling her. It was calling for a change, one she couldn't yet fathom, yet undeniably leading her.

25
Wise Man

NOT LONG AFTER, Shero came upon another teacher. She stumbled upon him quite unexpectedly, days later climbing some hills in Ecuador. He was an old man, a Wise One, a shaman who was sitting at the top of a small mountain.

He looked at Shero as she approached and said, "Welcome. I've been waiting for you. You have much to learn; are you ready?"

Without knowing anything about him or where she was or where she was going, she replied, "Yes! I've been looking for you forever, it seems."

"I've been here all along – waiting for you. Please sit down."

She sat and remained there for three years, only returning down the mountain periodically for supplies. This old man was called Wise One Alcivar.

"Close your eyes and travel with me," he said.

She closed her eyes and immediately was transported in time and space to a field of brilliance, to a place that had no name and no location.

Once there she was asked, "Are you willing to serve creation?"

"Of course, I said yes to this question years ago."

"Then you'll be asked to surrender everything."

"Okay, I have nothing, anyway."

"You will be surprised at how many attachments you still have. But we will take one step at a time."

Then in an instant a laser type beam came from nowhere and entered her heart. It pierced her, so hard and fast that she fell back. In the beam itself, her heart burst wide open, so far and wide that it turned inside out on itself. What was left in the place of what was formerly her guarded and protected heart was pure brilliance, pure light, pure radiance.

The presence of love stunned her. It was as if she were being transported to another realm, to another dimension. "This is love," the voice said. "This is bliss — and this is not the destination but the journey to awakening. To awakening to the truth of who you are and who you are becoming. This is your new normal."

And he left her there, stunned beyond words, opening, expanding, receiving. She fell back on the ground and was filleted wide open; all that had protected her dissolved; all the places she carried wounds came into her awareness. All the vows and contracts she had made with the universe and herself came into her awareness, almost like the commandments on the tablets.

"This is what you have created; this is your own making. The work now is to come into bliss and allow; to surrender all

that is unlike love. It won't necessarily go easily. It won't go without a fight.

"Surrender… it's the last and most impossible thing to do until you do it. Then it appears easy and of course, surrender would be the answer to your prayer; the answer and the action no matter what. It is the Spirit within you that does the work.

"This is what you have created as your persona, as your protection, as your ability to function in this world called humanity."

Then the light shone even brighter, washing over her, blinding her, scouring the tender insides of her heart and blessing her with love.

The bliss she felt in this moment was beyond her wildest dreams. "Oh, this is for what I have come. This is living. This is Oneness with love and light; joy and peace." She was wordless, she was thoughtless; she was emptied and full at the same time. Emptied of thought, emotion, reaction. Full of light, full of love.

When the experience came to an end the Wise One, Alcivar, looked at her with kindness, compassion and a depth of understanding. "Yes, you are the one," he said, "the one I've been waiting for. We have work to do. Go and rest now; return to me at first light and we will begin."

Shero stumbled off and came to a small cabin; it was more like a room than a cabin, but it had a bed and a bit of food. She collapsed on the bed, still altered from the experience, and flew; she went back into her altered state and soared around creation. She looked and saw; she could see the planet Earth and other places she could not quite make out. She realized she was not alone; that there was something so much greater than her and the life she'd been living. She caught a glimpse of the beauty; a glimpse of the freedom and fulfillment that could come to her.

Then she slept – or at least went unconscious.

The next morning, she woke at first light and wondered where she was and what had happened to her. Was it real, was it a dream? Was it happening in the world or just in her head?

She went outside and saw the beauty of the countryside. She had not noticed it before, with all the variations of colors and textures. It was as if her vision had attained high definition. Years earlier, she had been able to see the energies of people, but not recently. Not since the big betrayal of her friends. Since then she had been blinded by her pain, by her loneliness. She continued doing good work in the world, but it didn't matter as much, because she was numb.

No longer numb, she witnessed glory. She fell on her knees and wept with joy. The tears flew freely, like a dam had been broken. They were tears of gratitude, of humility; then the tears of her pain began to flow, and she wept hard, loud heart-wrenching sobs. Then the tears turned again. They were the sweetness of heartbreak transmuted to love, transmuted through pain and suffering into acceptance and love.

Shero looked around at the mountain she was on, part high plains, part forest and so beautiful. At the edge of the forest she caught glimpses of wildlife. She saw deer, birds, rabbits and then a raccoon. He was looking directly at her, and with eye contact, she remembered having a raccoon friend, named Mask, in her journeys as a child. Mask gently recognized her and welcomed her to that time and space. She knew she was in the right place at the right time.

At that moment she was ready to find the Wise One. She approached and sat at his feet. He took her places without ever leaving his seat. He exposed her to the brilliance of the universe and the darkness of humanity. She experienced the cosmos and the inner world. Each time they were together, she learned, and she grew.

She began to expect and experience that the expanded bliss she experienced would lead to the hardest work ever.

Shero would land in a place of brilliance and Oneness to be filled with a pure essence of love; then moments later be crashing into an emotion that was within her. Almost without notice, she would be scared, so fearful that she could hardly breathe, suffocating under the density of some emotion or belief.

Alcivar would stand by her and say keep surrendering, keep breathing, keep letting it go. Transcend the emotion for love. Let it rip you apart as it exits your consciousness; let it burn through the cells of your being as it is consumed and transmuted.

Just as she thought she was emptied out once again, the cycle would continue. In between, the Wise One would teach her about the universe, the cosmos. Most of the teaching came in few words if any. It was brilliant and agonizing at the same time; both exhilarating and excruciating.

The moment came one day when from an expanded place of love came the memory of abandonment. She was stunned by the force with which it arrived. "It is time to forgive," came the message.

"No! I will not forgive – they hurt me so deeply and changed my life. I will not forgive them." She of course was thinking of her friends Bill and Jill. Her reaction stunned her, as she had already done a magical forgiveness process with them. She thought it was done and complete. She said to Alcivar, "I did forgive them, so why did I just tell you I hadn't? It was that forgiveness process that led me to you. What's going on?"

Wise One Alcivar said gently, "You did indeed do a layer of forgiveness, on the human level, yet there is more. It's deeper than your friends; it's humanity and soul levels of forgiveness that are being called for now. You will go no further without it. What you have seen as possible is only possible through true and complete forgiveness.

"Forgiveness is giving up the expectation of a better tomorrow. Forgiveness is giving up the burden that you carry so you can feel and be more love. Forgiveness is neither condoning nor forgetting. Forgiveness is what is called for.

"Go away and contemplate this moment. Consider forgiveness and what it may take from you and what gifts it may give you. Feel into and journey into a life of forgiveness and then consider the other side, continued life without it. Notice what you notice and return when you are ready."

Shero felt ashamed and embarrassed at her reaction and yet knew the truth of his words as they resonated through her being.

She also realized at this point that it was only the full and complete truth that could set her free. She could not fake this one, she could not fake it until she made it. It had to be true; it had to be full; it had to be fully felt and transmuted.

She took to her favorite perch outside her cabin and became willing to journey to the places within that were unforgiven; willing to see with new eyes and willing to become even more willing.

She returned in memory to the betrayal of her friends, allowing the old memory to jumpstart her deep dive into new layers. Feeling it as it burned through her being, fighting it as they did her wrong, what they did it to her. She accessed the victim role that she stood in and realized that she could indeed go no further carrying the victim energy.

She did the work as she'd been taught to access the energy and follow the thread of that to the core of its inception or origination. She followed victimhood first; the ways she was a victim to her life, and she was shown how many, many times she felt that and how it played out.

In judgment of herself she was appalled by the number of times she was victimized. Shifting to judgment she began to process that; the judgments she had held against others; Jill, Bill, her parents, all the people who did not understand her and finally, judgment against herself. That was a big one.

Shero had to process all of it; let it burn, see it, feel it, and remain willing to surrender judgment to the greater love. She wailed, she cried, she screamed at the injustices she lived through and she remained willing; or at least willing to be willing.

She wailed her pain away, with the sound carrying the energy from the cells of her being. There were places in her body where the energy was stuck, and she returned to the Wise One for assistance.

He had her lie down and he placed his hand on her abdomen, he pushed and pushed, prodded and pulled energy, dark energy, from deep in her system as she wept and wailed her pain away; finally falling into a deep, dark, still sleep.

When she woke there was more. The judgment was gone, but there was more story, more memory to process. She kept going. Noticing what she was being shown, taking it deep into her experience, feeling it through, and following the threads that came.

She processed anger, betrayal, fear, judgment. She found shame mixed in, along with blame and being a victim. She went all the way back to her infancy and not being understood by her parents. It was painful; it took time. Lots and lots of time. It took support and the removal of energies by the Wise One.

She kept at it with a vague memory of the love and bliss she had experienced. She could not find them, could not reach them, but trusted they were there, buried under the dark energies and that they would appear once again.

She kept diving in again and again. Her tenacity was profound. Her commitment to getting to the other side honorable. She sat with her teacher, she prayed, she screamed, she wailed, she wept, and she even begged.

"Let it stop. Make the pain go away." In the depths of those prayers she heard, "The pain will stop when you quit resisting it. The emotions will come to an end as you process through them completely. You are doing great and you are not alone."

"I feel sooo alone," Shero wailed.

"We know; we are with you always," she heard in the depths of her being.

"There is an end and it will be beyond your wildest imaginations. Keep going, keep digging, keep surrendering. You are in the darkness now and there will be light again. We promise."

She did not know what the voice was, but she trusted it. And she kept going. The anger that overtook her became shame. The shame burned through her for months. Every little thought triggered more shame. She had shame that she was experiencing anger and rage again; that she could not move through it; that she must be a fraud. The shame that overtook Shero threatened to drown her in misery.

She asked the Wise One, Alcivar, "Why am I so filled with shame? Where does this shame come from?"

"It is yours and it is your ancestors; you are processing shame that is rampant in the cells of humanity on this planet. You are doing the work so that others who are not as strong as you can do theirs. You are feeling and releasing shame for all of humanity. You can do this. Keep surrendering. Let it burn and choose love instead. Let it overtake you and choose love in the middle of it. Let the shame burn and scream and flow like the lava of a volcano. Look at the lava flow and let it burn away from you all that is related to shame, rage, anger, even irritation, because it is all the same energy, the same frequency. Shame is a poison on the universe. Let the lava of love eat it up. Let the lava eat up anything and everything that is unlike love that is left in you."

Shero had once watched a video of an active volcano, its lava eating houses. The lava was slow moving and as it progressed, the house disappeared into it. Lava can be as hot as 1,600 degrees so anything and everything in its path gets eaten, disappears, melts, disintegrates, vanishes like a marshmallow in a campfire flame left too long. It simply burns off the stick and disintegrates into the flames.

She had watched an entire house being eaten by the lava; in a moment, there was something and then there was nothing. It was awful, it was outrageous, it was destructive, in a very calm manner.

She heard, "Let the lava of Spirit consume you and like a Phoenix you will emerge anew. Keep going. Keep breathing. Keep allowing and most of all keep surrendering! Surrender it all to Spirit."

So she kept going and going and going. Asking for support when she needed it; trusting that the Wise One was wiser than she and that he was leading her to something different; to something greater; to a something she didn't even know what to expect, but something.

And one day the shame was a bit less; there was space in the process. On that day she began to feel lighter; almost filled with a possibility of a newness. On that day she journeyed once more into the light. She was gifted a respite and rewarded with the blissful, light-filled journey to the ends of creation and beyond. She was given a vision.

It was a vision of what is possible when love reigns; when love overcomes fear for all time. She was shown her role in the awakening and healing of the planet. She was given a glimpse of what is possible and what was necessary. In that vision she was also given the strength and courage to drop any resistance she still had.

She was shown how her very resistance to surrender was causing much of her pain and suffering. She discovered that beneath rage was love. That beneath fear was love. She was shown that love truly is the only truth and it is our attachment to the lesser and denser emotions that holds them that binds them to us.

Shero saw how she had been justified, righteous, and defensive; that was the glue that held the emotions in a pattern of "stuck." She realized that if emotions are stuck, they remain in our body and wreak havoc, creating chaos in our thinking, in our physical bodies and in the thought process as well.

She understood that emotions are not good or bad, but stuck emotions are always a challenge. In this new realization Shero was able to let go even further; to absolve herself of the guilt of being resistant, of the guilt of being so filled with rage.

She was freeing herself in her willingness to look, see, tell the truth, and then feel the feelings. At that moment, her process shifted.

She became the willingness she was calling forth. She let the shame burn through without judgment or resistance; she let the anger burn until it fizzled out; she allowed the feelings of betrayal and abandonment to simply flow through her.

With no story about it, with no expectation of anything other than love, Love appeared. Love surfaced, as if it had been there all along. It was then that Shero was finally able to experience true forgiveness. It was at this time that the vision of her friends had come to her and forgiveness washed across her being at depth.

Love prevailed and she began to relax again. She stretched every day, she walked every day, she continued to process the thoughts, beliefs, and expectations she discovered every day until there was no more.

She was empty. She was thoughtless, emotion-less; she was mindless, and she returned to sit at the feet of the Wise One.

"Now what?" she asked. She was told to sit still for a while, bask in the emptiness for a time. To enjoy the moment of contentment, fulfillment and bliss.

"You have done splendid work and a great and mighty work it has been. Sit here in my seat for a time, I'm going on vacation. I'll be back in a couple of weeks."

And there she sat, at One with all that was. Allowing anything and everything to flow through her awareness.

And the people came. First, she was afraid, "I'm not qualified to be here as a Wise One," she thought, but she felt the fear and opened her heart. She sat with the person and when she left, they were both blessed. She sat by herself for a few more days.

Shero was in awe and wonder at what had transpired in the years she'd been on the mountain. She felt like a new person; certainly not the same angry, victimized woman who showed up at the feet of the master.

Another person came. Together they talked; she left radiant with a glow around her entire being. Then came another and another. Each person came with a desire to know love, so love she was and love she gave. It became easy; enjoyable, and she looked forward to the company every day.

Soon the time had passed and Alcivar reappeared. "Job well done, my good and faithful student. You are free to go."

"Go – go where?" Shero stammered as panic set in. "But I like it here – I want to stay right here for all time We do well together and I'm comfortable here."

"You did not do the work to become comfortable, my dear. You did the work so you could return to the world and do your mission to assist in the awakening of the planet, one soul at a time."

"But I don't know how," she whined, surprised at how quickly her confidence waned.

"Of course you do," replied Alcivar, "simply be who you are here to be. Simply stay connected to the greater awareness of All that is, and you will do fine. I'll be here, and you can reach me by simply thinking of me."

"But where will I go?"

"Follow your heart."

"But what will I do?" Shero fumbled as she recalled her earlier times of wandering the world, lost and alone.

"You'll know when you know. Trust the process. You are well prepared and now are graduating into the next level of transformation – and it will come. Remember your lessons; surrender anything and everything that is unlike love or neutral. Do whatever it takes to surrender, sooner than later; it becomes easier in the end. You are following a path laid out long before you arrived here on the planet. Now go forth and do your work. You are beloved, you are loved, and You are love."

···26···
Leaving Alcivar

AND OFF SHE went...

Into the world once more, with nothing but a small backpack and her peace of mind. Nothing in her consciousness but an empty willingness to allow life to show up as it does.

She met strangers on the road; she shared meals and stories. She talked with the people she met, and she was well cared-for. There was an easy adventure and simplicity to her days as she traveled along, still almost in a trance state; still almost in an altered place. She stayed in South America for a few months, listening each day to the wisdom guiding her. Paying close attention to the inner impulse that was sometimes very quiet, other times loud and clear.

On her journey, every day she spent time with the infinite, time in the silence and stillness. There was a sense of peace, of fulfillment. She was content with her life.

Shero remained a bit unclear about her mission and why she was here and continued to be alone on the journey, but it was okay. She trusted a divine plan that was un-seeable. She trusted herself and the universe and all was well in her soul.

Each day she gave gratitude to the wisdom that guided her and appreciation to the energies of the Universe – to the Time spent with Wise One Alcivar. He had become the most important presence in her life and was ever present with her.

If she had a question, all she had to do was stop, get still, ask, go into the silence and there he was. Ever present, ever presence. Loving, supporting and encouraging.

••• 27 •••
Humanity is Tough

AFTER WANDERING FOR a few weeks, Shero resumed her work and was called to assist a new village. She spent most of her time with the local people and loved it. Yet the agency she worked for had now initiated weekly virtual meetings. Shero found those to be laborious, at best. They were about checking-in and receiving missions but periodically they would address a personnel issue or be assigned global projects. During the meeting one week, Shero had bumped heads with another field agent as they were assigned to collaborate on a new project. They were fundamentally at different ends of the spectrum of the work and she knew she was being stretched yet again. In her process and with the intention of clearing herself so she could be more present with the team member, she ran. Shero had always enjoyed running for the physical benefits but even more so as it put her in a space where she could sort out her feelings without her egoic mind getting in the way.

After running a mile or so, Shero felt better. She had been struggling with some kind of partly hidden emotion and had been feeling "off." She removed her shoes and went straight out into the ocean. She swam out beyond the cresting waves and then rested. She was in her perfect place, surrounded by the wild; supported by the ocean, bouncing, bobbing, and basking in the glory of the process she just experienced.

She reflected. This humanity stuff is tough. She wondered why she could still get so triggered. It seemed like the more she expanded, the more she leaned into being her purpose and living her passion there would arise a second force. It stopped her in her tracks and distracted her from what she really wanted. She wondered if it was distraction or something else? She pondered these things while floating on the waves.

As she gently held the thought, as she explored these latest ideas with curiosity and without attachment, she noticed something. Every time she was expanding, something came that wanted to distract her. It could be an outer situation like the one with her co-worker, but more likely it was the inner process she had that was triggered by the outer.

"Is it distraction?" she wondered again. "Or could it be the next step, the next growth, the next quantum-leap in my consciousness?" She put on the lens of curiosity around the situation with the co-worker earlier in that week. What happened? How did she respond? What did she learn? And she kept diving deeper into the exploration.

As she unpacked each step along the way, she noticed that the distraction was calling her to be different, to think differently, to act differently than she had in the past. Because it was unfamiliar, it triggered an old past response. That was the indicator. What if she caught herself as soon as the indicator showed up? What might have happened then?

She continued exploring, not with judgment, but only wonderment and a sense of inner adventure. What could she discover? Then she saw it. She saw the patterns like lights popping in her brain.

She realized that the outer distraction is exactly that, the indicator of something different or the potential of something different happening in her internal world. The indicator is just that, a call to pay attention. An invitation to listen deeply both to the outer and to inner world. As she expanded, as she desired a different outcome, there was something within that needed to change.

As the lightbulb went off, she realized her desire for an empowered team, for better communication and synergy within the planning process. When her colleagues did not listen, or hear her, Shero was triggered. It wasn't about them, it was about Shero's ability to speak her ideas in ways that needed to be more clearly communicated.

She suddenly had another wave of inspiration wash over her. She felt her inner energy field do a restart, an upgrade; the clarity of what she'd been trying to explain was downloaded in an updated version.

She wept tears of gratitude. She loved this part of her life; not the pain that came before the breakthrough, but the breakthrough moment, when everything changed. She loved the newness, the understanding that poured into her. She loved her life and she loved this world in which she lived.

Right that moment, a dolphin swam by her. Jumping, twirling and even offering a spin in celebration. She'd always loved dolphins and knew they had messages for her. Shero swam alongside the dolphin for a bit, offering love, appreciation, and gratitude.

···28···
Shero Returns

SHERO HAD RETURNED to the States. She was following the impulse to find Jill and Bill; it had been close to a decade since she had any contact with them. She didn't even know where they were. "Where are they? How are they?" she wondered. She was a bit afraid to reach out to her friends, ashamed, somehow, at her actions and the realization that she had abandoned them without a thought, care, or conversation. The story she had made up was that they abandoned her, but when she realized, through her forgiveness process, it was only her story, and not even close to the reality, she knew she had to find them, to make amends and to apologize. She had just up and disappeared one day. Now she yearned to find them.

She followed the breadcrumbs of Spirit, followed the impulse that led her from South America back into the

States. From one state to the next she meandered with an end goal in mind, but no real hurry, direction or knowing of how to find them, trusting in divine timing.

Then one day almost a year after her final surrender process in Ecuador, she reached out and called the number Jill had had as a student a decade earlier – just on a whim, doubting there was any likelihood she would answer. She probably had changed her number many times since then.

One ring, two rings, the third ring and Shero was about to hang up, when an out-of-breath Jill answered, "Hello.…"

Shero was quiet, almost speechless at hearing her old friend's voice. She was silenced by the moment, not having a plan of what to say.

"Is anyone there?" Jill asked. "I can feel someone, but I can't hear you. Who is it?"

"Jill …" Shero said quietly.

"SHERO!!! Is that You? Oh my gosh, where are you? Are you okay? What in the world happened to you so long ago? You are on my mind every single day. I've been praying to find a way to find you.

"You know, I was so angry with you for disappearing like you did but one day about a year ago, I had a vision; it was like magic. Something came over me, all my anger disappeared. Then I could hardly remember why I was mad in the first place and there was only love and hope of well-being. Ever since then I've been praying to find you.

"Where are you?"

Shero told her and as it turned out she was only a few miles away. They arranged to get together in a few hours. It was surreal; Shero was excited and terrified a bit at what she might find beneath the warm welcome. She went to a park and sat on a bench.

Shero was overcome with affection for her friend and relived the moment of surrender on the mountain top in Ecuador several times over. She suddenly saw new waves of connection, new pathways she hadn't seen before. She was washed over and filled with love, grace, and gratitude for the infinite Spirit that guided her into the jungle, up to the mountain top and onto her healing awakening process.

And now, to finally see her friend again, to finally come full circle and discover what might be next.

She sat there in gratitude, in awe and wonder as she watched the sky change colors. She saw young lovers holding hands, walking in the park. She witnessed children playing and mothers calling them; she saw dogs and cats; older people, and young ones. All with renewed eyes of love.

···29···
Meeting Again

AS SHERO GOT ready to meet her friend, once again the memory of the journey through and to the Star Seed Planet was fresh on her mind. She was open and receptive, feeling a sense that something big was about to happen; something surprising and delightful was near at hand. She was not exactly nervous, but a bit jumpy, not knowing how the evening would unfold. Shero walked up the walk and tentatively rang the bell. Jill ran to the door, threw it open, and gushed all over her! She welcomed her home like a long-lost sister. She fussed and cooed and loved on her. Then Bill came home from work.

Shortly after Shero disappeared, Jill and Bill had married and had been building a life together. Now, Bill was a bit more stand-off-ish, he was wary; over the course of the evening, he began to soften but it would take him longer to open once more to Shero. Talking over each other, the girls laughed and cried and tried to catch up, while Bill watched. He was always amazed at how these two women could finish each other's thoughts and especially now, a decade since they'd seen each other. The three-some was restored. The locusts that had stolen the time from them would soon disappear.

The doorbell rang. Jill said, "Oh Shero, I didn't tell you – we have a daughter, a beautiful little girl, she'll be five in a few days. She's been with my mom today and that will be her coming home. She is quiet and different, so don't be concerned if she ignores you."

Bill went to open the front door and to inform their daughter that they had company.

Judith was a shy child, withdrawn, reserved and bright. Jill and Bill could see that she lived between the worlds and they always hoped that she would not be too sensitive, not too inner worldly, too other-worldly. They lived with concern about their beautiful, sensitive child and tried as best they could to protect her and keep her safe.

She was a child who would sit on the sidelines and observe. She never approached a stranger and it took her a long time to warm up to anyone, even her own grandparents.

Yet that night she walked into the room holding her grandmother's hand and stood for a moment. She looked at her mom, then her dad, then shifted her attention to Shero. Predictably, she would have left the room at that moment, without a word, but instead, to the great surprise of both her parents and grandparents, Judith walked directly into Shero's arms and exclaimed, "I've been looking for you. You're the one I've been waiting for. I didn't think you were real."

Afterword

Shero's Journey is a spiritual adventure – the first in a trilogy. Shero is our heroine and as it turns out, she was seeded from a different dimension. She doesn't know it, yet she must embrace humanity in order to be able to serve humanity in the great grand scheme of healing planet Earth. She faces dragons and chasms as in any hero's journey, but hers are of emotions – anger, rage, fear, terror, and shame. As she navigates her life on earth, she discovers the deeper meaning of life; she meets her challenges with strength and in the end, she realizes her mission, which is the very beginning of Book Two.

About the Author

For More Information about Aliza, you may visit her: http://www.Divine-Awakening.org/Alizas-Links/

Touching hearts, freeing souls and transforming lives. Aliza Bloom Robinson, vibrational catalyst, speaker, best-selling author and minister is committed to the Awakening of the world – which will result in the rise of love, purpose, passion and connection.

Aliza is the author of *Paradox of Awakening – Finding Peace in a World of Chaos; Falling Into Ease – Release Your Struggle and Create A Life You Love*, it's companion, *Falling Into Ease Guidebook – Simple Everyday Practices to Release Struggle and Create Ease; Be a BOA, (Bold, Outrageous, Authentic) Not a Constrictor* eBook; *and What is Mine To Do…? A Guided Process for Spiritual Discernment* eBook.

Find her on Amazon here - [amazon.com/author/Aliza]

She is a contributing author in the Best Selling 365 Series: *365 Ways to Connect with Your Soul; 365 Moments* of Grace; 365 Life Shifts; A Coaches Collaborative and to Thrive Magazine and Medium Magazine.

Aliza loves to travel, lead spiritual retreats and spending time with grandchildren! Aliza and her husband split their time between Arizona and Arkansas.

Aliza loves to hear from her readers! Email her at Aliza@Divine-Awakening.org

www.ingramcontent.com/pod-product-compliance
Lightning Source LLC
Chambersburg PA
CBHW030219100526
44584CB00014BA/1351